College–School Collaboration: Appraising the Major Approaches

William T. Daly, *Editor*

NEW DIRECTIONS FOR TEACHING AND LEARNING
KENNETH E. EBLE, *Editor-in-Chief*

Number 24, December 1985

Paperback sourcebooks in
The Jossey-Bass Higher Education Series

Jossey-Bass Inc., Publishers
San Francisco • London

William T. Daly, (Ed.).
College-School Collaboration: Appraising the Major Approaches.
New Directions for Teaching and Learning, no. 24.
San Francisco: Jossey-Bass, 1985

New Directions for Teaching and Learning
Kenneth E. Eble, *Editor-in-Chief*

New Directions for Teaching and Learning is published quarterly
by Jossey-Bass Inc., Publishers.

Correspondence:
Subscriptions, single-issue orders, change of address notices, undelivered
copies, and other correspondence should be sent to Subscriptions,
Jossey-Bass Inc., Publishers, 433 California Street, San Francisco,
California 94104.

Editorial correspondence should be sent to the Editor-in-Chief,
Kenneth E. Eble, Department of English, University of Utah,
Salt Lake City, Utah 84112.

Library of Congress Catalog Card Number 85-60841

International Standard Serial Number ISSN 0271-0633

International Standard Book Number ISBN 87589-774-6

Cover art by WILLI BAUM

Manufactured in the United States of America

Ordering Information

The paperback sourcebooks listed below are published quarterly and can be ordered either by subscription or single-copy.

Subscriptions cost $40.00 per year for institutions, agencies, and libraries. Individuals can subscribe at the special rate of $30.00 per year *if payment is by personal check.* (Note that the full rate of $40.00 applies if payment is by institutional check, even if the subscription is designated for an individual.) Standing orders are accepted.

Single copies are available at $9.95 when payment accompanies order, and *all single-copy orders under $25.00 must include payment.* (California, New Jersey, New York, and Washington, D.C., residents please include appropriate sales tax.) For billed orders, cost per copy is $9.95 plus postage and handling. (Prices subject to change without notice.)

Bulk orders (ten or more copies) of any individual sourcebook are available at the following discounted prices: 10–49 copies, $8.95 each; 50–100 copies, $7.96 each; over 100 copies, *inquire.* Sales tax and postage and handling charges apply as for single copy orders.

To ensure correct and prompt delivery, all orders must give either the *name of an individual* or an *official purchase order number.* Please submit your order as follows:

Subscriptions: specify series and year subscription is to begin.
Single Copies: specify sourcebook code (such as, TL1) and first two words of title.

Mail orders for United States and Possessions, Latin America, Canada, Japan, Australia, and New Zealand to:
      Jossey-Bass Inc., Publishers
      433 California Street
      San Francisco, California 94104

Mail orders for all other parts of the world to:
      Jossey-Bass Limited
      28 Banner Street
      London EC1Y 8QE

New Directions for Teaching and Learning
Kenneth E. Eble, *Editor-in-Chief*

Contents

Editor's Notes

For much of their recent history, American institutions of higher education have kept their distance from elementary and secondary education. That distance has increased with the growth of higher education since World War II. The prime activities and values of research universities are farthest removed from public schooling. Normal schools, which earlier in the century were close to public schools in number and relationships, have for the most part become liberal arts or general purpose colleges or universities. Often within higher education institutions, education departments or colleges are separated from other departments by attitudes and values echoing these larger separations.

In the wave of public school reform of the past decade, closer school-college collaboration has gained increasing attention. The Carnegie Foundation for the Advancement of Teaching has renewed its traditional view of education as a seamless web and of the need for schools and colleges to work together. Speakers at the 1984 national meeting of the American Association of Higher Education called an equal-status relationship between professors and schoolteachers an essential for successful collaboration. The collaborations described in this volume are examples of the diverse activities now underway nationwide.

The arguments for closer relationships begin with the irrefutable one that public schooling is the source for all our future mathematicians, doctors, and writers. What happens to students before they get to college is vital to what happens to them there and after. This simple fact has been brought home with great force to the sciences through the shortage of public school teachers in science subjects. Why are so many students ill-equipped to pursue scientific careers? Why do those who opt for scientific careers shun becoming public school teachers? It is no accident that many of the school-college collaborations have grown out of the disciplines of science and engineering.

But arguments for cooperation and collaboration go beyond that. They include several needs: to raise the status and morale of public school teachers; to assist public school teachers in keeping up with rapidly expanding and changing fields of knowledge; to help college professors be more effective teachers; to help students make more effective use of the years they spend in formal schooling; to reduce educational overlap and duplication; to provide a more effective transition between high school and college; to identify and assist both disadvantaged and gifted students at crucial points in their educational progress; to provide stimulation and motivation specifically for high school seniors and college freshmen; and to provide for all those engaged in education the benefits that cooperation and collaboration entail.

This volume is designed as a *user's manual* for those who might be interested in undertaking a college-school collaborative effort. It is designed to provide a *realistic overview* of the burgeoning national activity in college-school collaboration.

The Overview

The representative programs in this volume were extracted from a review of all the available compendia on existing collaboratives. From that very long list, ten major *approaches* to collaboration were identified, and more detailed information was solicited from a more limited number of programs of each type. The final stage in the selection process involved choosing one collaborative to represent each of the major approaches. My hope is that this use of representative case studies will provide readers with a readily digestible overview of this rapidly growing and very diverse area of activity. For readers who want to explore a particular approach in greater detail, additional examples of each of the major approaches are provided in the closing chapter on "Additional Resources."

The New Jersey Basic Skills Assessment Program, treated in Chapter One, is perhaps the most elaborate and sophisticated of the testing programs that have been adopted by a number of states in an attempt to define the nature and extent of the gap between college expectations and high school preparation—the gap that has provided much of the impetus for the collaborative movement.

The next block of chapters deals with programs in which colleges work directly with pre-college students. The University of California-Berkeley's MESA Program, discussed in Chapter Two, is a large and highly successful example of collaborative programs that focus on the early identification of promising middle and high school students—often minorities or potential majors in mathematics and science—and on providing the early support services necessary to increase the number of such students who gain admission to college and succeed there. These programs, however, usually stop short of offering credit-bearing college courses. Syracuse's Project Advance, detailed in Chapter Three, is the premier example and model for a number of collaboratives that go beyond early identification and support to offer college courses to pre-college students. Project Advance courses are, however, not directly offered by or at the university. Rather, the university helps to prepare high school teachers to offer those courses in their high schools.

Johns Hopkins Center for Talented Youth, discussed in Chapter Four, is the premier program and national model for those collaboratives that take the next step by directly organizing and staffing special college-level courses for pre-college students. Most of these programs, like the Johns Hopkins program, are designed for talented youth. The LaGuardia Middle College High School, discussed in Chapter Five, is a nationally recognized example of programs that take the final step in high school-college collaboration—the construction of a unified educational institution that combines high school and college. It is noteworthy not only as a pioneer of this approach to collaboration, but also because it, unlike most collaborative programs, is designed not for advanced students but for students already identified as likely drop outs.

The second major block of chapters treats collaboratives that work not with pre-college students, but with their teachers. From the point of view of potential participants, the National Writing Project, outlined in Chapter Six, constitutes a readily available opportunity for affiliation for those institutions interested in improving writing instruction. It is also a well-established national model for programs that seek to affect the maximum number of students by training teachers to train other teachers. The Academic Alliances Program, treated in Chapter Seven, is a newer but rapidly growing national network that also offers to interested institutions an opportunity for affiliation with a going concern without having to start from scratch. This collaborative, however, brings teachers together around their shared disciplines. It is about the business of building for teachers the kind of collective responsibility for the quality of disciplinary education that county medical and legal associations have provided for those professions.

The Yale-New Haven Teachers Institute, discussed in Chapter Eight, is also concerned with enriching content instruction. But it is perhaps most notable for its success in bridging what most would have viewed as the unbridgeable gap between the faculty of a high-powered research university and the teachers in an urban school district. The Stockton Connection, examined in Chapter Nine, also deals primarily with content instruction, but differs from the Yale collaborative in two major ways. Its constituency is drawn from a large, predominantly rural, geographic region in south and central New Jersey. And its emphasis on continuous content updating, designed to render the latest research developments in major curricular areas intelligible and interesting for classroom use, means that its offerings are determined more by current developments in the major areas of knowledge than by the expressed needs of teachers.

The final chapter, on the University of Missouri-Kansas City's relatively new Metropolitan Area Schools Project was selected less for the specific programs it supports than for the highly sensitive mechanism it has developed for identifying and responding to the multifaceted needs of area schools. For readers moved to the brink of action by the rest of the volume, it seemed an extraordinarily good model for getting started.

The Realism

A good user's manual should provide an overview that is not only comprehensive but realistic—one that treats obstacles as well as opportunities, failures as well as successes. For that reason, with a few exceptions, the selected collaboratives have been in the business long enough to wear some of the bloom off the rose. I also explicitly asked this pre-selected group of veteran contributors to address problems as well as possibilities. While the subheadings of the various chapters are not all identical, all of the contributors responded to my request that they deal, somewhere, with: (1) the origins of the project, including blind alleys; (2) its objectives, including those that turned out to be unrealistic; (3) a description not only of the current structure and activities of the collaborative but also of the evolutionary process that brought it to this point; (4) a summary of available evaluative information, not sanitized too much; and (5) explicit recommendations and warnings for readers who may be considering involvement in a collaborative effort.

It is, of course, a little much to ask contributors, who have poured a good chunk of their professional lives into these collaboratives and may still be involved in promoting them, to "come entirely clean" in print. To their great credit, they have, for the most part, managed considerable candor, and have thus saved us all from the boredom of reading straight public relations pieces. The rest will have to be left to critical readers to ferret out on their own.

William T. Daly
Editor

*William T. Daly is professor of political science
at Stockton State College, chairman of the
New Jersey Task Force on Thinking Skills,
and the founder and director of
the Stockton Connection Collaborative.*

PART 1.

Defining the Need

*New Jersey's statewide testing program demonstrates
that systematic data collection and reporting can have
a major impact—both on understanding the gap
between college expectations and high school
preparation and on the college and pre-college efforts
to close that gap.*

Testing and Reporting on Graduates: The New Jersey Basic Skills Assessment Program

Anthony D. Lutkus

In the mid 1970s there was a growing realization among New Jersey college faculty and administrators that "things were not the way they used to be." Replace "things" with "students" and you have the gist of their complaint. Scholastic Aptitude Test (SAT) scores had been falling both nationally and within the state. New Jersey's nineteen open-admissions two-year colleges were founded between 1967 and 1969 and their graduates entering the four-year institutions were not inspiring faculty confidence. Those few four-year institutions that had placement testing programs were observing a growing need for remedial sections of writing and math courses. These concerns were finally brought to the State Board of Higher Education, which decided that the existence and extent of the problem needed to be systematically assessed. The New Jersey Department of Higher Education (1977) resolved:

    1. That a New Jersey Basic Skills Council be established;
    2. That the Council develop a basic skills test;

W. T. Daly. *College-School Collaboration: Appraising the Major Approaches.* New Directions for Teaching and Learning, no. 24. San Francisco: Jossey-Bass, December 1985.

3. That all public colleges be required to use the Council's or a comparable test to assess entering students' basic skills;
4. That all public colleges develop remedial programs to meet the needs of their student body as indicated by those test scores;
5. That all public colleges report annually to the Council on the character and effectiveness of those remedial programs.

The Basic Skills Council, consisting of twelve faculty members and administrators representing the various sectors of the state's higher education system, worked cooperatively with the College Board and with the Educational Testing Service (under contract) to develop a test—the New Jersey College Basic Skills Placement Test (NJCBSPT). A full-time staff of three was assembled within the New Jersey Department of Higher Education to support the Council (Morante and others, 1984a, 1984b).

Since 1978, when it was first administered, more than 350,000 students have taken the test. In addition to public college students, the students of eleven independent colleges have been also tested. The test is not an admissions test. It is required after students are admitted to college but before they register for courses. The purpose is, first, to help place entering students in appropriate college courses and, second, to provide a statewide measure of the basic skills proficiencies of New Jersey's entering college freshmen.

Test Results

The NJCBSPT results indicate that thousands of students entering colleges across New Jersey lack proficiency in basic academic skills. While this problem is most pervasive among students from urban districts, it is prevalent in suburban and rural districts as well. The entering freshmen for the fall of 1984 displayed the following levels of proficiency in collegiate basic skills:

- 26 percent appeared to be proficient in verbal skills
- 28 percent appeared to be proficient in computation
- 12 percent appeared to be proficient in elementary algebra.

Clearly, these percentages of "proficient" students are distressingly low and, in fact, have changed very little over the past five years. For example, over the five years from 1980 to 1984, the percentage of students judged proficient in verbal skills has ranged within a narrow band from 26 percent to 29 percent. And the percentages of proficient students in verbal skills and in computation even declined by 3 and 2 percentage points respectively from 1983 to 1984, after small gains had been reported for 1983 in the verbal skills and in elementary algebra. While proficiency in elementary algebra held steady in 1984, it held steady at a meager 12 percent.

Recent High School Graduates. Initially, some raised the hope that recent high school graduates' scores might have been pulled down by students who had left high school some time ago and, therefore, might not be an accurate reflection of the skills of current graduates. This hope has been dashed. Of the 46,465 students tested in 1984, 62 percent (28,846) were graduates of the high school class of 1984. Similarly, recent graduates made up 63 percent of the entering class in 1983. The pattern of proficiencies for these students is not very different from the total population of test takers: 28 percent appeared proficient in verbal skills; 35 percent appeared proficient in computation; and 16 percent appeared proficient in elementary algebra. These recent graduates also showed the same slight decline from 1983 to 1984 in verbal skills (-3 percent), and in computation (-1 percent).

The test results indicate, at best, *no improvement* over the last five years in the preparation for college of recent high school graduates entering New Jersey public colleges and universities. Over the last few years, surveys of the extent of observed need for college remedial work done by City University of New York (1983) and the National Center for Education Statistics (1985) suggest that New Jersey's percentages of proficiencies seem too harsh only when the lack of standardized testing permits the colleges the luxury of subjective judgment, but on target where colleges systematically test their entering classes.

High School English and College Proficiency. The NJCBSPT form collects data on several student background variables including self reports on the number and type of high school math and English courses taken. Ninety-seven percent of these recent graduates have taken four years of English. Yet, of these, only 29 percent appear proficient in verbal skills. With less than four years of English preparation the "appear proficient" category drops to 11.6 percent. Thus, "four years of typical high school English courses do not guarantee adequate preparation for reading and writing at the college level" (Lutkus, 1985b).

High School Mathematics and College Proficiency. The relationship between high school math courses taken and subsequent proficiency in elementary algebra and computation suggests that any preparation of less than four years of math virtually ensures a lack of proficiency in elementary algebra. Of the 1,825 students who took only one year of algebra in high school and the 1,634 students who took one year of other math, only *one* student scored high enough to "appear proficient" in elementary algebra. Even among the students who took the typical "college prep" program of Algebra I, II, and Geometry, only 3.3 percent were proficient in elementary algebra. Specifically, there were 6,831 students in this category and only 228 scored at least 25 out of 30 elementary algebra questions.

Students who completed the "college prep" sequence plus calculus were much more likely to be proficient (66.3 percent) in algebra. Less than 10 percent of the recent graduates (2,266 of 24,141), however, fell into this category. These results have been similar for the last five years.

One welcome trend is that more of our recent high school graduates are taking the fourth year of math. In 1980 students who took the math sequence through calculus made up only 3.9 percent of the test takers. In 1984 this group had risen to 6.2 percent of the test takers. Were it not for this small increase in the size of the calculus-taking group, the statewide proficiency levels in elementary algebra would have decreased over the last five years.

The impact of the Basic Skills Council's mandated testing of college freshmen, and of the test results just described, has been rather dramatic on college remedial instruction but slight on the high schools.

The Impact of Statewide Testing and Reporting

Within the Colleges. The testing program in New Jersey has been followed up for four years by statewide analyses of the effectiveness of the remedial programs in the colleges. The extensive data on student outcomes required by the Department of Higher Education seems to have raised the priority level of remedial programs in the eyes of college administrators. Almost all of the colleges have undertaken the reallocation of effort and resources necessary to comply with the directive that they test all entering students and provide remediation for those who need it. In addition, required reports on the structure of advisement, counseling, learning centers and content of remedial courses have stimulated program improvement. Most recently, data have been collected from the colleges on two cohorts of full-time students: those who entered in the fall of 1982 and persisted for four semesters, and those who entered in the fall of 1983 and who had completed two semesters as of the end of spring 1984 (Lutkus, 1985a).

The most important finding was that skills instruction can be effective even when it is undertaken as late as the college years. Specifically, skills-deficient students who complete the appropriate remedial course sequence have a far greater chance of college success than skills-deficient students who do not complete remediation. Indeed, having followed such "remediation-completed" full-time students over four semesters, we can report that their subsequent academic performance is acceptable, even when compared to that of non-remedial students. The data from the outcome measures in this study indicate the following:

1. Retention rates are actually *higher* at the end of both two and four semesters for those students who *complete* remediation than for better

prepared students who *did not need* remediation at all. Seventy-five percent of state college students and 55 percent of county college students who completed their remedial sequences were enrolled in the fourth semester compared with 69.8 percent and 51.5 percent of non-remedial students in the respective college sectors. The pattern is similar at Rutgers and the New Jersey Institute of Technology, which have more selective admission standards. However, skills-deficient students who do not complete their remediation within four semesters stand little chance of college success. For example, of the 2,090 full-time county college students who had not completed remediation in writing within three semesters, only 22 percent were still enrolled in the fourth semester. Of the 643 students in the state colleges who had not completed their remediation in writing at the end of three semesters, 35 percent remained at the fourth semester.

2. The successful survival rate (a ratio of the original cohort who both remain *and* have at least a "C" average) is similar for students who have completed remediation (57.8 percent in state colleges, 37 percent in county colleges) and for those who did not need it (62.8 percent in state colleges, 39.8 percent in county colleges). However, the successful survival rate is only 28.8 percent for state college students not completing remediation and 12.5 percent for county college students who did not complete remediation by the fourth semester.

3. Students who complete their remedial sequence in the state colleges by the fourth semester are an average of *five college credits behind* their peers who did not need remediation (48 versus 53) at the end of the fourth semester. In other words, in exchange for a "credit gap" or temporary slowing in progress toward the degree, the students who complete remediation benefit from a preparation that gives them virtually the same probability of passing college-level courses as that of non-remedial students, and of having success survival rates two to three times higher than students who did not complete remediation.

4. Finally, virtually all institutions reported significant gains in student scores on pre- and post-course testing in their remedial courses. Despite these score gains, however, not all students who passed a course actually reached the minimum test score that would have placed them out of remediation in the first place. The percentage of students passing remedial courses who met that criterion varied enormously from college to college—from a low of 49 percent to a high of 100 percent.

The Basic Skills Program has recently begun to follow up this statistical reporting with site visits to particularly effective remedial programs. The point of such visits is to discover the dynamics of programs that work and to share the results both with other colleges and with the high schools.

Finally, each sector of public higher education in New Jersey (two-year colleges, four-year state colleges, and Rutgers University) has evolved a council of faculty and administrators who are intimately involved with remedial programs or institutional research. These groups now meet regularly to follow the policy issues and reports from the statewide Basic Skills Council. They serve as vehicles for inter-college communication and as a source of feedback to both the Basic Skills Council and the college presidents.

Within the Schools. Reports on the statewide test results and the effectiveness of the college remedial programs are made public and are widely covered by the press and television in the New Jersey/New York metropolitan area. Written statements of expectations for college-level proficiencies in reading, writing, and mathematics are also made public not only to high school administrators but also to teachers, parents, and students. Finally, by agreement with the Department of Education the NJCBSPT scores are mailed to high school principals along with interpretive materials and a summary of statewide results. Principals are requested to discuss the test results with their school boards.

In a number of workshops with principals, and in checking with school boards and organizations such as "Schoolwatch," however, we have found that this strategy works in theory but not in practice. Some principals report that even though we give them detailed reports by student on the placement test results, they do not know how to use the results to change their curriculum. More disconcerting is the problem of principals who simply "file" the printouts and never bring the results to their school boards.

Some help in this regard may be on the way, however, in the form of a new High School Proficiency Test initiated by the New Jersey Department of Education (the department responsible for kindergarten through high school). Even though this test is set at a ninth-grade level, it differs from the test it replaced in that it is designed to measure at least some of the same higher-level skills measured by the NJCBSPT. And, because students must pass the test before they can graduate from high school, it will probably capture the attention of school administrators in a way that our test results have not.

Between Schools and Colleges. Over the eight-year history of the NJCBSPT, hundreds of college faculty members have served on the three test development committees and as essay readers during the scoring of the essay portion of that test. High school teachers also serve in both these capacities and the cross-fertilization that has occurred as a result has helped to build good will both for the testing effort and for high school-college relationships in general. In addition, a series of workshops on the testing program for principals, and for math and English curriculum supervisors has helped to foster better understanding of the relationship between college expectations and high school curricula. One concrete example of the results of this informal contact between high school and college teachers is that holistic scoring of student essays has spread from the scoring sessions for the NJCBSPT to both college English final exams and high school writing courses.

Similar collaborative efforts have also developed in math. In response to the basic skills test results, the state colleges in New Jersey raised their minimum math entrance requirement from two to three years, and efforts are now underway to help the schools improve math instruction. Professor Charles Pine, 1985 CASE National Professor of the Year and chair of our math committee, has worked with high school teachers to develop a ninth-grade algebra curriculum that is partially based on error patterns discovered from NJCBSPT research and that emphasizes quantitative thinking. Pilot implementation of this Ford Foundation sponsored project was successfuly carried out by sixteen school districts during 1984-1985, and interest in this curriculum is growing in the high schools since the ninth-grade statewide High School Proficiency Test also emphasizes "higher-order" thinking skills in mathematics.

Finally, in its attempt to reconcile admissions access with academic excellence, the New Jersey Department of Higher Education has chosen the strategy of distributing additional funding to New Jersey colleges via competitive grant programs. Several of these grant programs have categories for high school/college articulation efforts and some focus, in particular, on in-service training opportunities offered for high school teachers by the colleges.

Lessons for Collaboration

The eight-year history of the NJCBSPT program carries two lessons for those interested in collaborative work—one of substance and one of method.

The NJCBSPT program began with the limited goal of assessing freshman academic competence in New Jersey. With the testing continuing into its eighth year, the lack of improvement in test scores has highlighted the need for the colleges and the state educational agencies to go beyond testing to work cooperatively with the pre-college community, not only in making expected college competencies clearly known but also in improving basic skills instruction at both the pre-college and college levels. Our test results have made it clear that there will be no "quick fix." Collaborations between college and pre-college communities will have to include the upgrading of teacher professionalism; improvement of standards in college teacher-education programs; a streamlining of high school curricula to emphasize basic subjects over electives; and consideration of drastic changes in "classroom" methods of educational delivery in recognition of the coming demographic shifts toward a preponderance of minority children in the schools. It is a very rare college faculty that sees a need to address these issues. But they must do so if they expect ever again to teach well-prepared freshmen the way "it used to be."

The formation of the Basic Skills Council itself also provides at least one important lesson as to method for those who seek to establish interinstitutional collaborative efforts, at whatever level. Statewide testing was viewed with trepidation in 1978. Would low test results be used to criticize the colleges? Would funding be cut for remedial courses if there were too many of them? Was testing a racist, exclusionary practice? Eight years later the placement testing program is an institutionalized operation that is seen as a part of every college's student entry process. The mechanism by which this transformation in attitude was achieved focused attention on the careful selection of the *people* who make up the Basic Skills Council. Each was and continues to be a respected figure on his or her campus. As a result, the policies of the Council were seen as coming from the Council, not from the state. Any start-up collaboration must have this "grass-roots" character or it will fail.

References

City University of New York. *Assessment and Improvement of the Academic Skills of Entering Freshmen: A National Survey.* Research Monograph No. 5. New York: City University of New York, Instructional Resource Center, 1983.

Lutkus, A. D. *Effectiveness of Remedial Programs in New Jersey Public Colleges, Fall 1982-Spring 1984.* Trenton: New Jersey Basic Skills Council, New Jersey Department of Higher Education, 1985a.

Lutkus, A. D. *Results of the New Jersey Basic Skills Placement Test, Fall 1984.* Trenton: New Jersey Basic Skills Council, New Jersey Department of Higher Education, 1985b.

Morante, E. A., Faskow, S., and Menditto, I. "The New Jersey Basic Skills Assessment Program." *Journal of Development and Remedial Education,* 1984a, 7 (2), 2-32.

Morante, E. A., Faskow, S., and Menditto, I. "The New Jersey Basic Skills Assessment Program: Part II." *Journal of Development and Remedial Education,* 1984b, 7 (3), 6-32.

National Center for Education Statistics. *Survey of Remedial College Courses.* Washington, D.C.: National Center for Education Statistics, 1985.

New Jersey Department of Higher Education. *A Resolution Establishing a New Jersey Basic Skills Assessment Program.* Trenton: New Jersey Department of Higher Education, 1977.

Anthony D. Lutkus is director of the New Jersey Basic Skills Assessment Program at the New Jersey Department of Higher Education. He is a cognitive psychologist who has written on child development, college instructional methods and college placement testing. He is also a 1985 Fellow at the College Assessment Program Evaluation (CAPE) project sponsored by the Fund for the Improvement of Postsecondary Education.

PART 2.

Working Directly with Students

*The MESA Program provides evidence of what can
be done with early and continuing intervention—for
students' motivation and performance levels in the
schools, and for the minority recruitment efforts of
colleges and universities.*

Early Identification and Support: The University of California-Berkeley's MESA Program

Mary Perry Smith

MESA began in 1970 as a collaborative effort between the University of
California-Berkeley, College of Engineering and Oakland Technical High
School. The program was started because an engineering faculty member
was interested in increasing the number of Black and Mexican-American
students enrolled in the College of Engineering. He received assistance
from the university's outreach staff, which conducted a series of interviews
to assess why students from these groups were not selecting engineering or
physical science college majors. High school math and science teachers,
along with Black and Mexican-American university and secondary students, were interviewed.

The Need

The students and teachers who were interviewed consistently
referred to three factors that they viewed as basic obstacles to increasing
the numbers of the MESA-targeted students who qualified for entrance to
university engineering and physical science majors.

W. T. Daly. *College-School Collaboration: Appraising the Major Approaches.* New Directions for
Teaching and Learning, no. 24. San Francisco: Jossey-Bass, December 1985.

First, for admission to the university, students were not required to complete trigonometry, chemistry, or physics. Even the revised 1986 admission requirements include three years of math, but *not* specifically trigonometry, and one year of a lab science, but *not* specifically chemistry or physics.

As a result, counselors, in an effort to help students meet the grade point average requirements for entrance to the university, often did not encourage students to take trigonometry, chemistry, or physics. Not only are these courses not required, they are also some of the most difficult high school courses, and, therefore, can seriously damage students' grades and their chances of being admitted to the university of their choice.

Because of these two factors, most of the college preparatory students from the MESA target groups, including those interested in careers in engineering and the physical sciences, dropped out of math before completing trigonometry. Lack of information about what it takes to major in one of the math-related fields made it nearly impossible for these students to know that trigonometry is a requirement for those persons studying in engineering and the physical sciences. When these students were not able to pass calculus—the freshman math class at UC-Berkeley— they changed their majors to non-math-related fields.

It seemed clear that both high schools and universities needed a program that would help more students from the target groups stay in advanced mathematics and science classes. These students also needed more contacts with university admissions office personnel and with role models from the math-related professions.

Description

High school students who are selected for the MESA Program must be enrolled in geometry and have at least one more year of high school to complete. They must also be from a MESA target group and express an interest in math or the physical sciences. MESA does not try to recruit students into the sciences, but rather supports existing student interests. The MESA Program has developed a core of student services for these students that directly address the needs that came to light during the initial interviews.

Academic Advising. This component provides students with information on admissions requirements for math-based college majors. Students receive assistance with course selection from the MESA adviser who is a math or science teacher at their school. The advisers work with students to ensure that they are prepared to pursue their interests in math and science. They see that students are enrolled in high school courses that will give them the maximum number of options for admission to a math-related major at a four-year postsecondary institution. Students who participate in MESA are required to study math at least through trigonometry. They are required to take chemistry and are encouraged to take physics. MESA staff also work with advisers to provide tutoring assistance to students on a regular basis at the school site to help the students maintain competitive grades in their math and science courses. Finally, study group activities are organized that focus on teaching students to broaden and deepen their understanding of the subject matter in each course.

Summer Enrichment Programs. Special summer programs provide MESA-targeted students with the academic and study skills necessary to make them competitive for college admission. These programs focus on academic courses in math, science, English, and computers to help students get a head start on the subjects they will take the next year, and to strengthen their understanding of the previous year's work. They also emphasize study skills assistance to help students develop sound study habits and learn how to use appropriate independent and group study techniques.

Scholarship Incentive Awards. These awards provide recognition to students who meet MESA's academic and scholastic standards. Students who achieve at least a B-plus average in trigonometry, chemistry, physics, and advanced English are eligible to receive cash awards each report period. MESA ties these awards to the particularly difficult math, science, and English courses students often avoid taking, and to SAT scores. The purpose is to motivate students to enroll in difficult courses and work for top grades.

Career Advising. This component provides students with current information about professional opportunities in math-related fields. Students go on field trips to industry sites and regularly hear speakers from math-related professions. This helps some participants get technical work experience and puts all the students in contact with professionals, some of whom serve as role models.

College Advising. This element of the program helps students understand the choices they have when selecting colleges and majors and assists them in completing applications for college admission, scholarships, and financial aid. MESA staff work with university and college admissions representatives and high school counselors to provide participants and their families with as much assistance and information as possible. Students have the opportunity to go on at least one field trip each year to a nearby university, and MESA graduates return to MESA high schools to talk about their college experiences.

Implementing the MESA Model

The model MESA has used to implement its programs is that of contracting with universities and colleges to provide MESA program components to schools in their areas. Specifically, the contracts are with colleges or departments of engineering, which receive *annual grants from MESA to hire a staff person whose sole responsibility is to implement the MESA Program components in the schools.*

MESA has found it effective to subcontract with colleges and universities that are interested in and able to provide MESA services to schools in their areas, rather than working with local school districts or community colleges, because these institutions help to make it clear that the goal of the MESA Program is to help students achieve a four-year college education in a math-related area. Further, having the engineering units of these institutions sponsor the program gives it the additional prestige students need to maintain their academic goals in the face of competing social and extracurricular interests.

The MESA Center is located at the sponsoring university or college and is staffed by a MESA Center Director. The center director works with school administrators to select an adviser for the program at each school site. The director assists the advisers in the selection of students who meet the MESA guidelines, then provides the advisers with the needed materials, information, and in-service and staff support. Specifically, MESA staff at the college center arrange speakers and field trips, help recruit and hire tutors, and provide funds for scholarship awards. They also work with industry representatives to provide services to the schools.

Each MESA Center works with six to twelve senior high schools. Recently the program has been extended to work with junior high schools. The Carnegie Corporation funded the Junior High MESA Program as a pilot project for 1984–87. This act reflects an understanding of the importance of early intervention into the math and science preparation of future MESA high school students. In the absence of such early intervention, less than 10 percent of MESA target-group students in any high school will be enrolled in the initial college-prep math class that qualifies them for MESA participation. The junior high program is designed to increase this percentage.

The MESA Support Team

We have already discussed the central figures in a MESA team. But in order for the program to operate effectively, a substantial backup team must also be developed, as described below.

Statewide Office. MESA has fifteen college centers in California.

They are supported by a statewide office and a statewide director, who works with program and research staff to provide services to the centers. This office has major responsibility for: collecting data on student participation and achievements from junior high school, through high school and college, and into their careers, and using that data to help raise funds to support MESA Centers; providing staff in-service and program evaluation in order to ensure quality control in program delivery, including regional workshops to recognize participating teachers and provide them with opportunities to share experiences; organizing and supporting regional contests and activities for MESA students; and developing and publishing the necessary handbooks, reports, and publicity brochures.

Universities. As already noted, each of the MESA Centers is affiliated with a university and has offices on a college campus. A member of the engineering faculty is appointed by the dean to act as a faculty sponsor who oversees the program's fiscal and supervisory functions and who hires and supervises the center director.

Industry. From MESA's first year, industry has played an important role in making the program successful. Inasmuch as MESA is working to increase the number of minority persons who enter math-related professions, industry participation is particularly important in legitimizing this objective. Support from industry is also critical financially. At least one-fourth of the annual statewide budget comes from industry donations, additional amounts are awarded each of the centers by local industries or divisions of larger companies, and industry often donates surplus and new equipment to science, math, and computer classes.

Industry executives serve on the statewide Industry Advisory Board, local Center Advisory Boards and the Industry Technical Advisory Committee. They assist MESA staff by providing direct access to such industrial resources as: career information published by the companies; field trips that help students become acquainted with the world of work and the variety of jobs that are performed in a particular company; speakers for MESA student and parent meetings; and volunteers to tutor, provide activities for study groups, and assist students to prepare for math and science contests. Some industries also offer MESA students summer jobs to help them gain experience in a technical field.

Secondary Schools. Schools are, of course, the MESA Program's base of operations. The approval of district superintendents, school boards, and principals is necessary before a MESA Program can begin. The success of the program, once established, depends on the support it receives from administrators, counselors, and especially the MESA adviser. Advisers work with MESA students in much the same way any teacher works with a high school group that he or she sponsors. MESA groups focus principally on academic rather than social matters. As indicated above, students learn what is needed to enter college, requirements for entering various professions, and what to expect as a working professional. They study together in support of their common goal of being competitive in applying for admission to collge. Ideally, advisers meet weekly with students to monitor progress throughout their participation in the program.

Parents are invited to orientation meetings when their children are selected to participate in MESA. They are kept informed about the program through newsletters and direct contact with advisers. At the end of the year, parents are invited to attend the graduation and awards banquet held at each center. Many of the centers have parent clubs that assist with study groups, fund raising, and supervision of field trips. Some centers provide parents' field trips, industry speakers, and workshops on financial aid and college admission requirements.

Finally, high school counselors provide MESA staff with important baseline data on school programs and populations, as well as student test scores and transcripts.

Evaluation

MESA now has sixteen university centers throughout the state of California, and enrolls over 4,000 students from 140 secondary schools. The program has been unusually successful. Nearly 90 percent of MESA graduates enter college, and more than 60 percent are accepted into a math-related college major.

The original program design was based on a careful review of suggestions from students and teachers, and only one fundamental program change has been necessary in MESA's history, that during its third year. That change was made in the guidelines for granting student awards. Originally, all MESA students were given a monthly stipend and the opportunity to earn additional financial incentive awards based on grades—in accordance with MESA's status as an incentive program that rewards students who meet its high academic requirements. Unfortunately, the students who received regular stipends did not perceive them to be rewards for hard work, so these subsidies did not serve the purpose of stimulating students to work for higher grades in order to receive larger awards. As a result, the stipends were dropped and all awards were tied to student achievement. Approximately 20 percent of eligible MESA students now earn one or more of these awards, and a majority of all MESA students compete for them.

Other program activities have been refined and augmented, and procedures have become increasingly standardized since MESA matured and expanded to a statewide program in 1977. Greater emphasis has been placed on the summer enrichment programs and the participation of parents as a means of addressing the great variation in academic program quality among MESA schools.

Conclusions

Several specific factors have contributed to the success of the MESA Program.

1. It is designed to serve a very specific need that is of concern to all parties involved—teachers, district administrators, target students, university faculty, industry, and parents.

2. With limited resources, it focuses its efforts and does not try to take on larger problems related to making changes in established educational institutions.

3. Its services are designed to supplement and complement what schools already offer, in a manner that helps students get the most out of their schools' courses and teachers.

4. It works with the schools' staff members who are most involved in the education of the participating students—math and science teachers.

5. It works out of sixteen centers located at universities that work directly with the secondary schools in their areas.

6. It pays the salary of a full-time staff person at each center whose sole responsibility is to implement the program.

The MESA experience also suggests some general recommendations for those interested in establishing collaborative projects.

1. Any collaborative program must involve the principal parties in planning and conceptualization.

2. Any program that involves a school must have the approval of the superintendent and the full cooperation of the site principal.

3. The purpose of a program must be supported by all collaborative partners and the design of the program must focus on that purpose alone.

4. The program must be cost effective, making the best use of resources from all involved parties.

Mary Perry Smith served as the first MESA adviser in 1970, and as statewide coordinator of programs when MESA expanded in 1977. She now serves as a member of the MESA board of directors.

Project Advance demonstrates the advantages of collaboration for dealing with "senioritis" among advanced students, for supporting teaching-oriented faculty development, and for conducting ongoing research on effective instruction.

Early Instruction in the High School: Syracuse's Project Advance

Bette C. Gaines,
Franklin P. Wilbur

Syracuse University's Project Advance is a collaborative program between the university and selected high schools that allows students an opportunity to earn college credit while they are in high school. The program also serves two other major purposes. It provides both in-service training for high school faculty and a continuing forum for communication between educators from both schools and universities. Finally, as an agency of the university's Center of Instructional Development, Project Advance conducts extensive on-going research and evaluation as part of its efforts to systematically improve instruction. The Project Advance staff manages the logistics of the agreement that permits colleges of the university to offer their regular courses to non-matriculated students in nearly eighty high schools in five states where the courses are taught by high school faculty who serve as adjunct instructors. These adjunct instructors are trained, evaluated, certified, and supervised by members of the academic department that offers the same course on the Syracuse campus. Now in

W. T. Daly. *College-School Collaboration: Appraising the Major Approaches.* New Directions for Teaching and Learning, no. 24. San Francisco: Jossey-Bass, December 1985.

its twelfth year, the program has received national recognition and has been duplicated or adopted by many other institutions. This suggests that the concept might be generally workable and beneficial to students, high schools, and universities (Wilbur, 1981; Wilbur, 1984). The emphasis on the continuing self-evaluation, follow-up of former students, and carefully documented supervision that has been part of the program since its inception provides a good deal of relevant information to those who might be considering joining or initiating a similar program.

The Initial Rationale

Superintendents and principals from seven Syracuse area high schools met on several occasions during the 1972 summer vacation to informally discuss their discontent with their schools' programs for college-bound seniors. They discovered that declining academic motivation and boredom, particularly among seniors planning to enter college, were common problems. They also found themselves under increasing pressure to ameliorate the situation and to provide some educational alternatives for students who were either electing early graduation or regressing academically.

With these common concerns, the high school administrators approached the Vice-Chancellor for Academic Affairs at Syracuse University, described the situation to him, and asked him whether there was anything the university could do to help. He found their observations persuasive and agreed that a solution should be worked out cooperatively. He asked the director of the University's Center for Instructional Development to meet and work with them.

The high school administrators' sense of the problem was echoed, at roughly the same time, in the Fleischmann Commission Report on the New York schools (1973) and the report of the Carnegie Commission on Higher Education (1973), both of which pointed to similar symptoms and to the inadequacy of existing programs for gifted students. Having college-bound seniors come to the university campus was quickly ruled out as undesirable for several reasons. The most obvious were logistical problems involved in accommodating the schedules of the two institutions.

Some of the high schools had already tried other alternatives: advanced placement, for example, and arrangements that brought college faculty into the high schools. But these alternatives were also judged to be inadequate or unsatisfactory. Advanced placement had served some students well, but for others it did little to improve day-to-day student performance, despite the efforts of talented and dedicated teachers and bright, highly motivated students. The alternative of professors coming to the school was unsatisfactory because the college faculty were available to students only during class time. The inaccessibility of the professors eliminated, for students in the classes taught by the visiting faculty, important individual attention. Clearly another approach was needed.

Syracuse University Project Advance (SUPA) evolved from these meetings and from subsequent discussions with high school teachers and college professors. Its development was facilitated by the fact that the Center for Instructional Development had provided resources for course development and evaluation efforts to be undertaken for some of the university's freshman courses.

This development included the printing of supporting materials and course outlines, which made these courses especially appropriate for the cooperative effort. Because the content and goals of these courses were clear, it would be easier to maintain college standards in the high school (SUPA) sections. After careful review of high school-college programs nationwide, a pilot version of Project Advance was constructed. Its design remains essentially unchanged today (Wilbur, 1981).

The freshman English course seemed a likely choice for the small pilot project because the Director of Freshman English, the chief developer of the restructured course, was also prepared to train and supervise the teachers who would offer the course in the high schools. The course itself was structured in a way that permitted students to move at their own pace, and student and instructor manuals were already available to guide them through the units of the course's six credits.

The English Department was also willing to support the program, if they could be assured that the high school instructors would offer the course without alteration that might bring into question the integrity of the transcript. The public schools agreed to select and send qualified teachers to be trained and to meet other conditions specified by the university. The first Project Advance students were among the graduates of the high school classes of 1974. Of the first six pilot schools in the Syracuse area, five continue to offer SUPA courses. The rationale behind the initial effort has continued to sustain it. The program now offers eight courses from two colleges of the university, involves nearly eighty schools, and serves approximately 3,800 students annually.

Objectives

The objectives that initiated the program were narrower than those that sustain it, and the benefits that have accrued to participants at all levels have exceeded any that were initially envisaged by those involved in the first tentative effort.

Public School Administrators. The objectives of the public school administrators in 1972 were, as already noted, to bring to their respective districts a program that would challenge the top 15 percent of their students who were not being adequately served by the high school programs in some disciplines. Some of those students were ready to begin college work in English, others in math or science, and still others in two or more areas. Growing interest in academically successful students, the restless political climate of the country, and the activism that had crept into the schools among student leaders combined to focus attention on the curriculum, and suggested that needs of the bright, motivated students were frequently not being met. The school administrators wanted a program that would appeal to these students, to their articulate parents, and to their faculty as appropriately challenging and interesting. Although the conditions of the 1980s differ from those of the 1970s, these academic concerns have not changed.

Students. For students, these academic priorities have both personal and economic aspects. Youth is a time of impatience, especially for the brightest. The brightest students are anxiously anticipating beginning their college programs, and the lack of challenge in course content during the senior year of high school is vexing at best. They learn quickly, and they are frustrated at slow pacing of instruction. Often these students' questions, inferences, and challenges are unwelcome or even viewed as disruptive. Indeed, they may actually become disruptive simply out of boredom. The challenge of doing college work and meeting college standards provides the stimulation that these students require.

Success in college courses for these students gives them the challenge that they seek, and satisfies, at the same time, their desire to advance academically. If they can earn credit in several courses, they may shorten the time required to obtain their baccalaureate degrees. Alternatively, many simply use their SUPA credits to gain early access to advanced college courses in areas of special interest. Thus while at least 60 percent of the students go on to graduate study, a much smaller percentage have used these credits to shorten the time required to receive undergraduate degrees (Mercurio and others, 1982).

For other students the program tests their ability to do college work, by giving them a taste of college requirements and standards. Not all succeed. But even those who do not succeed seem to agree that the experience is beneficial in giving them a realistic appraisal of their readiness. These students also report that SUPA helped them to develop study habits and skills that served them well in further college study (Wilbur, 1981; Mercurio, 1980; Lambert and others, 1984).

The University. For the university the first objectives were limited, and they have remained so. The willingness to serve the needs of the adjacent community motivated the project from the outset. While an element of excitement must have motivated the first small staff of graduate assistants at the Center for Instructional Development as they carried out the initial logistical aspects of running the program, a simple humanitarian desire to help meet a perceived need was the primary motivation for the first faculty member involved. A small amount of seed money to support the teacher training program and supply texts for the trainees came from the state. The university may well have realized that public relations benefits would derive from the success of the project. But the arrangements for the relative independence of its operation and the separation of its operating budget suggest that the innovation was not designed to recruit students for the university. Indeed, it does not appear to do so.

High School Teachers. But what draws the high school teachers to SUPA? The high school faculty who have sought training and certification to teach the course have proven to be strong, independent, and purposeful. Like their students, most of them seem to be attracted primarily by the challenge presented by the college courses. They undertake the responsibility of teaching in the Syracuse program because they want to work with students who challenge them, in a program that stretches and strengthens their own pedagogical skills. Some are also curious to learn exactly what college will require of their students so that they can adequately prepare their other college-bound students for the freshman year.

University Faculty. The university faculty members who are the campus supervisors and mentors of their colleagues in the high schools resemble all these other groups. They seem to welcome the challenge imposed by something new. They clearly enjoy the interchange of ideas and the professional growth that derive from involvement in the program. They report that they are refreshed and stimulated by their discussions with students and teachers in the high school sections.

What all of these participating groups and individuals seem to have in common is a desire to make education better.

Mechanics

The present structure of Project Advance is similar to its original structure, but it has expanded to meet the demands of the present levels of enrollment and has been modified as a result of experience (Wilbur and Chapman, 1978). For example, the number of people required to provide logistical support is larger, and their jobs are more specialized. The SUPA coordinating staff includes a director, three associate directors, a records director, an office manager, two word-processing specialists who share a single position with additional responsibilities for travel arrangements, a receptionist-typist, an evaluation intern, and one or two work-study students.

The primary responsibility for administration of the program is the director's. He is assisted in his responsibilities by the associate directors. Each of them works with faculty in one or more courses. One of the associates has the additional responsibility for evaluation projects. The associates are expected to assist the faculty in arranging for their visits to the schools, parents' and students' orientations, the summer training workshops for adjunct faculty, reports of supervisory visits, and related correspondence. Most of the communication between the university and the participating schools is handled by the associates or the director. Their close cooperation with the faculty and easier accessibility makes them effective proxies for the professors in most matters not exclusively academic.

Most important in the working structure of the program is the direct contact and communication between the supervising faculty and their colleagues in the schools. Visits are made at least once each semester to each of the schools. These visits include meetings with students, administrators, and guidance personnel; but their primary purpose is to review student folders and to confer with the adjunct instructors in a collegial, helping relationship that ultimately determines the success of the cooperative effort. Following the visits, the supervising faculty member files a confidential report of the meetings and observations held in the schools— this to inform future visits—and writes to the instructor and administrator to confirm the principal points of the discussion and any conclusions that may have been reached. In addition, campus faculty members are available as guest lecturers or as advisers on curriculum planning at the secondary level. Conversely, the talent pool represented by the high school adjuncts has been tapped by the university for consultants on instructional material design, and to fill various campus teaching asignments.

Evaluation

A considerable quantity of resources and energy is devoted to program evaluation and research on instruction. This evaluation effort is important in maintaining the integrity of the program and in communicating to supporters and potential participants sufficient information about the courses and students to help them make carefully considered decisions. Questions addressed in research and evaluation projects sponsored by SUPA have included the following:

1. Are the specified college standards being properly maintained? Can SUPA tell other institutions that grading and learning experiences on- and off-campus are equivalent?

2. Is the academic credit students earn easily transferable to other colleges and universities?

3. How effective are the course materials, general structure, and content sequence? What teacher behaviors and course characteristics seem to best facilitate learning?

4. What kinds of students are being served by the program and how do SUPA participants do in college? What are the long-term effects on the students' academic performance?

Standards. A number of studies have helped to establish the comparability of performance between students in college campus and high school sections of the same courses. In chemistry and biology, we have also compared the grades earned in Project Advance sections with grades on Advanced Placement examinations in the same subjects. Project Advance students have consistently performed as well as or better than their peers on college campuses (Mercurio and others, 1983; 1984a; 1984b). Also, the grades earned in SUPA courses proved to be good predictors of Advanced Placement test scores.

Credit. A series of follow-up studies were instituted during the first year of the project to determine how SUPA courses would be received by the colleges that admitted SUPA students. The results indicated that the majority of SUPA students had received credit and exemption from similar courses.

Effectiveness. The Classroom Behavior Survey (Chapman and Kelly, 1984) is given annually to students in each course offered in a two-semester sequence and once each semester to students in single-semester, three-credit courses. The survey is not an evaluation of teaching, but a descriptive instrument in which students respond on a four-point Likert scale to items that describe the instruction, content, and structure of the class. The printouts of the data are transmitted to the teacher in a summary that analyzes the class response. An extra copy of the analysis is available for the teacher to share, but copies are not directly available to the public school administrators. Teachers who are experiencing problems in class response to instruction often find the survey helpful in identifying the cause of the problem. Conversely, in the absence of problems, the survey helps teachers to confirm their sense of how the class is perceiving their experience.

Success in College. We have recently conducted studies of former students following their completion of college programs, in an attempt to profile the students as a group and to learn how well their Project Advance experience had served them throughout their degree programs. Details of these reports are available from Project Advance (for example, Mercurio, 1980; Mercurio and others, 1982). In general the students agreed that the courses had served them well, and that their grades had predicted well their subsequent college performance.

Of course, the supervisory visits described above are also a form of intra-institutional evaluation, a kind of healthy self-examination that is particularly useful in articulation arrangements. Every evaluation effort undertaken by Project Advance has either demonstrated the strength of the model or led to its improvement.

Reflections: Recommendations and Warnings

In the early years of Project Advance, its staff worried about the ominous warnings that educational innovations seldom last for more than five years. Several staff members undertook studies of innovation itself to find out what produced that gloomy observation. Among the important characteristics of successful innovations were self-evaluation and adaptation, and a sense of ownership on the part of the participants.

Evaluation. A child of Syracuse's Center for Instructional Development, Project Advance early established mechanisms for self-evaluation, some of the results of which are summarized above. The number of those evaluation reports that have been published and widely disseminated indicates the extent of that commitment.

Ownership. The project was initially less sensitive to the importance of ownership than it now is. Early introductions were made to public school administrators, and they in turn decided to adopt the program and appointed or recruited teachers to come for training. As a result, the program was viewed by faculty in some schools as an administrator's program that had been imposed on them as a burden.

Because of Project Advance's increased sensitivity to this need for a sense of ownership on the part of the high school instructors and their academic departments, early discussions about course offerings now include the probable instructors and other members of their departments. Involving so many people means that more time—usually a year—elapses between initial consideration of the course by the high school and commitment by both institutions. Most participants will agree that this is a helpful delay, one that prevents misunderstandings that might otherwise occur.

Educational Validity. Perhaps the most important warning that can be given is that the cooperative arrangement, if it is to survive, should be undertaken because the participants are convinced that it is educationally important—that it is good for the students it is intended to serve. It must not be simply a recruiting device for the college nor a way of occupying the time of instructors who would otherwise be idle.

Long-Term Support. This approach to collaboration also requires continual reinvestment of capital: to maintain the support services; to pay the supervisory, administrative, and support staff; to pay for travel to the sites; to provide scholarship assistance to needy students, in-service training for teachers, and the like. The tuition that students pay is used to support and expand the program as a self-supporting agency of the university. That financial independence is also an important factor in its success.

Personnel. This model is also fragile in the area of personnel. The success of the program depends on the interest and enthusiasm of college faculty and, in particular, on their willingness to travel to the high schools, to meet with the adjunct instructors there, and to work with them in the workshop and in-service training seminars, while still carrying their full load of campus responsibilities. The program depends, too, upon the support of school administrators who can ensure the conditions necessary to offer the program. The departure of a supportive administrator creates a period of uncertainty. Teacher transfer and retirement can also disrupt a successful program if the school has not trained sufficient teachers to fill the gap. Often, too, internal political turmoil in a school means that extra efforts must be made by the sponsoring college to nurture and sustain the cooperative program.

Conclusion

Despite differences in professional training, work environment, and the reward systems of their institutions, high school and college teachers and administrators can and must find ways to work together. The Syracuse University Project Advance experience with joint programming has demonstrated that traditionally disparate school systems can collaborate, even on a large scale. Collaborative efforts of this kind require commitment, energy, and careful attention to detail at every step. But they are enormously rewarding. Collaborative efforts bring students the challenge and opportunity for growth that whets their appetite for more learning and reinforces their belief in their ability to undertake and succeed in college work. And they bring together for growth and increased effectiveness the teaching professionals from their respective institutions.

References

Carnegie Commission on Higher Education. *Continuity and Discontinuity: Higher Education and the Schools.* New York: McGraw-Hill, 1973.

Chapman, D. W., and Kelly, E. F. *Classroom Behavior Survey: Administration and Interpretation.* Syracuse, N.Y.: Syracuse University, 1984.

Fleischmann Commission. *The Fleischmann Report on the Quality, Costs, and Financing of Elementary and Secondary Education in New York State.* Vol. 2. New York: Viking Press, 1973.

Lambert, L. M., Ruiz, L., and Chao, C. I. "The Transfer of Syracuse University Credit Earned through Project Advance: The Class of 1983." *Project Advance Research Report,* Spring 1984.

Mercurio, J. "College Courses in the High School: A Follow-Up Study." *College and University,* 1980, *56* (1), 83–91.

Mercurio, J., Lambert, L., and Oesterle, R. "College Credit Earned in High School: Comparing Student Performance in Project Advance and Advanced Placement." *College and University*, 1983, *59* (1), 74–86.

Mercurio, J., Schwartz, S., and Oesterle, R. "College Courses in the High School: A Four-Year Follow-Up of the Syracuse University Project Advance Class of 1977." *College and University*, 1982, *58* (1), 5–18.

Mercurio, J., and others. "Performance of Project Advance Students on the AP Biology Examination." *The American Biology Teacher*, February 1984a, *46* (2), 106–108.

Mercurio, J., and others. "Project Advance and the Advanced Placement Program: A Comparison of Students' Performance on the AP Chemistry Examination." *Journal of Chemical Education*, April 1984b, *61* (4), 377–378.

Wilbur, F. P. "High School-College Partnerships Can Work." *Educational Record*, Spring 1981, *62* (2), 38–44.

Wilbur, F. P. "School-College Partnerships: Building Effective Models for Collaboration." *NASSP Monograph*, 1984, *68* (473), 14.

Wilbur, F. P. and Chapman, D. W. *College Courses in the High School.* NASSP Monograph Series, Reston, Virginia: National Association of Secondary School Principals, 1978.

Bette C. Gaines is an associate director for Syracuse University Project Advance with major responsibilities for faculty training and field supervision.

Franklin P. Wilbur is director of Project Advance, and professor in the graduate school of education at Syracuse University.

*The Center for the Advancement of Academically
Talented Youth demonstrates the contribution that
colleges can make to the education of students who
are ready for a level and pacing of instruction not
readily available in the schools. Its success also reflects
the burgeoning demand for such instruction.*

Early Instruction
by the College:
Johns Hopkins's Center
for Talented Youth

William G. Durden

Within the last two years one national report after another has examined
the state of American education and, all too often, the results have been less
than positive. Low teacher salaries, lack of coherent curricula, inadequate
student performance, high student and teacher dropout rates and irregular
local, state, and federal funding have made the American response to educating its youth a very uncertain affair. Among the remedies often proposed is
a closer working relationship between schools and colleges. It is hoped that
through such arrangements or partnerships educators can begin to rectify
some of the lingering difficulties of the American educational system. One
major structural difficulty is that often two-thirds of the last two years of
high school and the first year of college are repetitious. This situation is
particularly damaging for some of our nation's most talented youth whose
time and talent we may be wasting during a crucial three-year period of
their intellectual and social-emotional development.

W. T. Daly. *College-School Collaboration: Appraising the Major Approaches.* New Directions for
Teaching and Learning, no. 24. San Francisco: Jossey-Bass, December 1985.

However, school-college partnerships, while they can appear to be enticing methods to improve the quality of American education, are not always so easily created or maintained. Any dialogue between disparate levels of the American educational system can automatically bring into play the "shadow politic" of our educational ethos: the belief that different degrees of professional respect are rendered to members of precollegiate and collegiate education by the American public; a supposed lack of university understanding of what is necessary to instructing and developing precollegiate youth; the belief that university persons will summarily disregard the intellectual and pedagogical contribution of precollegiate teachers in a school-college partnership; the belief that a college's involvement in a school-college partnership can be attributed only to economic motivations, that is, robbing the cradle to meet financial needs at the university. This shadow politic is a powerful reality. It must be kept clearly in mind and confronted directly by anyone wishing to undertake a collaborative project.

It might be instructive therefore to examine carefully a school-college partnership that has been considered highly successful—The Johns Hopkins University Center for the Advancement of Academically Talented Youth (CTY)—and, through that examination, to identify both those critical components that have contributed to its success and those features of the effort that are still impaired by elements of the shadow politic.

CTY—A General Description

The Johns Hopkins University Center for the Advancement of Academically Talented Youth has gained national recognition for identifying and educating mathematically, scientifically, and verbally able youth. In 1971 the university pioneered a successful method of finding and helping talented adolescents with the founding of the Study of Mathematically Precocious Youth (SMPY) (Stanley, Keating, and Fox, 1974; George, Cohn, and Stanley, 1979; and Benbow and Stanley, 1976). Today, the Johns Hopkins Talent Search model and the academic program developed by CTY have been replicated in other schools, colleges, and universities both in the United States and abroad. The rationale underlying CTY's efforts is based on three beliefs: (1) that talented youths should have an opportunity to fulfill their intellectual aspirations regardless of the age at which their abilities first appear; (2) that those talented youths should have an opportunity to advance educationally according to their individual rate of learning and level of performance; and (3) that talented youths should have an opportunity to appropriate curricula that have been organized to respect a natural sequence of learning.

This rationale is now reflected in a comprehensive response to the education of academically highly able youth, consisting of three programmatic initiatives: (1) an annual talent search and recognition for seventh-grade students in public, independent, and parochial schools throughout the world; (2) academic programs for precollegiate youth on weekends during the spring and fall and for extended lengths of time during the summer; and (3) research and evaluation. The comprehensive program also provides a series of supplemental services, including tutorial-by-mail programs, assessment and evaluation services, a training institute for educators and parents, courses for parents, young student classes (seven to eleven years of age), and academic counseling services. This agenda involves the university in working directly not only with educators and parents but also, and primarily, with precollegiate youth (Durden, forthcoming).

Origin

The Johns Hopkins University did not begin its initiative on behalf of highly able youth as a self-generated institutional priority, but rather as a response to a community initiative. In 1969, a sixth-grader in the Baltimore schools was recommended by a member of the community to take a summer college course in computer science at Johns Hopkins. It was apparent to the young man, his parents, and his teachers that the sixth-grade science and mathematics curriculum was not challenging him sufficiently. Indeed, this estimation was accurate, and he proceeded to earn the highest grade in his college class while still a sixth-grader. The college professor, in turn, noted the extraordinary capabilities of the young man and directed him to the attention of Julian C. Stanley, professor of psychology. As a result of testing and conversation, the young man, with the consent of his parents and his school officials, entered The Johns Hopkins University as a full-time student at the age of thirteen. At that time, there were no transition programs such as CTY. This young man received his bachelor's degree in mathematical sciences at seventeen, his master's degree in mechanical engineering three months later, and, subsequently, a doctoral degree in Computer Science at Cornell University. He is currently on the staff of Cornell University and is an international authority on computer theory.

Professor Stanley felt that there must be other students in the United States for whom the regular curriculum was not appropriate either in pace or in level of instruction. He began a modest research project in 1971 to conceive of ways in which he could effectively identify these students. Some key decisions were made early. Stanley would concentrate on identifying those talents that would reflect the particular strengths and educational capacities of the parent institution (The Johns Hopkins University)—mathematical and scientific reasoning abilities. He would favor a system of identification that was psychometrically valid and economically feasible. He would subject all his efforts from the beginning to stringent research and evaluation. And he would address the young students directly in all correspondence and appeals.

As a result of his initial attempts, Stanley discovered that there were indeed many other students needing an education different from that provided in the regular curriculum, not so much in subject matter as in pace and level of instruction. As a result of this discovery he began modest-sized classes in precalculus mathematics on weekends at The Johns Hopkins University, using pedagogical principles that permitted students to concentrate on what they clearly did not know rather than repeating what they already understood. A system of pretesting, prescriptive instruction, and posttesting was initiated. Nationally normed, standardized examinations were used in all situations. To interest identified students in this educational opportunity, Stanley made his appeal directly to the students themselves, thereby requiring of them a major role in their own educational planning from the start. In addition, the classes offered at the university on weekends were characterized by an overt effort to offer curricula readily available in the schools, but adjusted to a different pace and level of learning. Stanley reasoned that the slow pace of instruction for youth with demonstrated talent in a particular field was a major contributing cause of the early boredom and frustration experienced by highly able students. He believed, therefore, that acceptance of a daily school regimen often characterized by a rigid lock-step system of kindergarten through four years of college, without variation for different ability levels, was ultimately irresponsible.

As a result of a number of scholarly articles in which he scrupulously documented his efforts, Stanley's approach to the education of highly able youth began to attract local, national, and international attention. However, what moved the effort from a small research project with SMPY to a large comprehensive public service and research/evaluation effort by the university was not initially a well-structured collaboration of school systems with a university. Rather, it was an effort that focused on the identified needs of individual young students. The response to those needs with a well-defined method of education attracted, gradually and indirectly, those individuals throughout the world—parents, school teachers, administrators, and concerned citizens—who also believed in the activities undertaken by SMPY and CTY. The initial effort, then, was directed toward assisting students and not toward involving school systems. The premise, to put it bluntly, was that getting too involved with comprehensively changing the system would only impede positive change in behalf of students.

As interest in Stanley's early efforts increased dramatically, and as the focus of the program expanded into the humanities, Stanley and the administration of Johns Hopkins acted to ensure the perpetuation of the initiative as an institutional feature. In 1979, Steven Muller, President of The Johns Hopkins University, established what is now CTY as an academic center reporting directly to the Provost and Vice-President of Academic Affairs.

Objectives

Students. Even though CTY has expanded the university's commitment to precollegiate education, the initial objectives of Stanley's work have been perpetuated. CTY continues to place the student and his or her needs in the foreground. The student continues to take responsibility for his or her own educational planning. And CTY's educational approach remains roughly the same. Mathematical and verbal reasoning abilities in youth are identified through the use of nationally normed and standardized examinations, often exceeding in intellectual level the chronological age of the youth. An educational agenda is then set which develops those talents concretely, by completing the coursework found in the regular curriculum but in a manner that respects the identified abilities of the child. In so doing, the lock-step of education, the artificial borders between elementary, secondary, and collegiate education are broken.

Schools. CTY serves the schools by offering them a clearly defined, well-documented method of proceeding with the education of some of their most highly able youth. It serves those teachers and administrators who are willing to join CTY in a reexamination of an educational system that has often placed its participants (students and teachers) in a position of serving time rather than learning. CTY does indirectly provide schools models, justifications, strategies for change at the local, state, and national levels, but the desire for this service continues to be self-generated.

University. From the university's point of view, CTY permits it to be engaged in yet another area of pioneering work, confirming the university's priority of charting new approaches, and new programs that maintain the best and most valued of inherited knowledge. In addition, the extensive publicity directed to CTY's efforts both nationally and internationally underscores the university's vision of itself as an international institution (with campuses in Baltimore, Washington, Bologna, Italy, and China, and alliances with other institutions throughout the world) serving knowledge and research. Finally, CTY's contact with precollegiate education keeps the university informed about those pre-college needs of student and teacher education that might render its own services at the undergraduate and graduate level more appropriate and timely.

Evaluation: Some Successes

The Talent Search. CTY believes that exceptional mathematical and verbal reasoning abilities among young students can be identified by a systematic and valid means: the talent search. Since 1979, CTY has identified more than 79,000 highly able adolescents through this method. The identification process relies on nationally-normed standardized tests, particularly the College Board's Scholastic Aptitude Test (SAT). Seventh-grade students (usually twelve to thirteen years of age) who score as well as the average college-bound high school senior on the SAT are eligible for specially designed coursework.

The talent search also allows students to assess their strengths and weaknesses in mathematical and verbal areas. "To see how well I do," or "To see what I need to work on" were responses given by over 50 percent of the 300 top-scoring students in the 1981 talent search. The self-evaluation made possible by SAT score reports and the compiled results of all participants encourage the students to carefully plan their education and adjust it closely to their specific academic aptitudes. In addition, every student who participates in the CTY talent search receives a certificate of merit applauding his or her high academic potential; an Educational Planning Guide to assist student, parent, and teacher in selecting appropriate educational experiences; invitations to various CTY counseling and career workshops; and a listing of summer and fall/winter opportunities for out-of-school educational opportunities. Top-scoring students are invited to attend award ceremonies and are eligible for one-course scholarships to attend local colleges while still in high school. The talent search thus extends well beyond the mere identification of academic talent, both by recognizing academic potential at an early age and by allowing teachers and parents to gain additional information to help students develop that potential appropriately during the remaining school years.

Academic Programs. CTY academic programs are distinctive both in their content level and in their pacing. Students not only have the opportunity to study challenging traditional subject matter (writing, Latin, Greek, physics, biology, and so on), they also can advance educationally according to their own pace and level of learning in an area of identified strength. For many young students, CTY provides the first opportunity to match achievement to ability. For example, in the math program, some students complete two to four years of high school math in just a few weeks. The key to this process is to discover initially what the students already know of math before they begin a subject such as algebra or geometry, and then to devise a course of study that focuses upon what they clearly do not know. In addition, many students advance to college-level math and obtain college credit while still in junior high school or high school, thus challenging the traditional sequencing of the learning process.

CTY's special attention to diagnostic and prescriptive instruction in math, the humanities, and the sciences not only accelerates the pace of education, it also provides an atmosphere in which students develop as independent, self-motivated learners.

Residential programs, established in 1980, provide the opportunity for talented students from all over the United States and abroad to come together at a college campus and pursue intensive academic and cultural activities. The programs are held in the summer and consist of two three-week sessions. Each class meets four to six hours per day, five days per week. Courses are offered in languages, expository writing skills, precalculus math, computer theory, and high school biology, physics, and chemistry. In 1980, 109 students from nine states and Washington, D.C., participated in one three-week session. In 1985, more than 2,500 students from forty-five states, Washington, D.C., and several foreign countries attended. The residential program is the most rapidly growing academic effort at CTY.

The commuter program component of CTY offers courses throughout the year that supplement the regular in-school education of those students identified in CTY talent searches. The courses are similar to those offered in the summer residential program and take place on weekends during the academic year and on weekdays during the summer. The commuter opportunity, originally offered only at the Baltimore campus of The Johns Hopkins University, has expanded to other parts of the country through satellite centers.

Academic programs associated with CTY do not attempt to teach "creativity." Rather, the task is to give form to the creative impulse. Here action is taken in historical context. Much creativity has been wasted in the absence of a form with which to represent it—for example, expository writing techniques, literary genres, symphonic modes, or mathematical formulation. For CTY, creativity naturally emerges for intellectually talented youths when the circumstances include substantive material for study, highly motivated students, and teachers who are both highly able in their subject and passionate about its instruction.

Students. CTY's proudest achievements are directly related to the accomplishments of the young students with whom it associates. This accomplishment is well-documented in the form of a series of longitudinal studies, but several anecdotal highlights may be appropriate here. In 1985, three of the top seven high school mathematicians selected to represent the United States in the International Mathematics Olympiad received part or all of their mathematics education through CTY's fast-paced coursework. In 1985, the second place winner in the International Science and Mathematics Fair Competition was a young person who received his math, science, and writing education in large part through CTY. Finally, in 1983, two fourteen-year-old CTY writing students had short stories accepted for an international anthology about growing up in America, published by the Rowohlt Publishers of the Federal Republic of Germany.

Teacher Selection. CTY searches the country for the most highly qualified instructors for its academic year and summer programs. Its basic criteria are expert knowledge in a particular liberal arts discipline, an ability to work with precollegiate students, and a sense of humor and of the outrageous. With these basic guidelines CTY seeks its staff from all levels of instruction—elementary, secondary, and college. And it is this healthy mix of teachers from all levels working for a common purpose—the education of youth—that helps break down some of those artificial barriers that often impede communication among various levels of instruction.

Evaluation: Some Problems

Robbing the Cradle to Fill a Freshman Class. CTY is sometimes accused that its efforts are merely a ruse to get qualified students to attend The Johns Hopkins University—the younger, the better. While such a charge might appear plausible at first glance, its validity disappears on closer examination. The Johns Hopkins University is one of those fortunate institutions of higher education whose pool of highly qualified applicants to the freshman class has been growing steadily for the last decade. The freshman class, which is limited to approximately 650 students annually, is chosen from several thousand candidates, only a small number of whom are associated with CTY. Under these circumstances, a talent search effort, dealing with tens of thousands of students and carrying a substantial price tag, would certainly be outrageous institutional overkill to fill a class of only 650 students.

Credit and Placement. CTY coursework often covers work treated in the local school, but at a more rapid pace and at a greater depth than instruction in the regular setting. Some schools, however, still refuse to accept student achievements in the CTY experience despite the careful documentation of progress through the use of standardized testing (that is, College Board High School Achievement and Advanced Placement Examinations). Some students who have successfully completed, for example,

Algebra I and II with CTY in a three-week intensive summer program, are required to repeat the program the following year in the schools. The shadow politic discussed earlier is manifested in the refusal of home schools to acknowledge individual differences and to believe that knowledge can advance more rapidly than is typical in the school system.

However, as CTY continues to publish data on achievement, not only during CTY programs but through longitudinal studies, the case is becoming more compelling for the acceptance of advanced placement or credit in the local schools. A recent survey of students returning from one of CTY's summer mathematics programs revealed that of the 144 students responding, 121 received appropriate credit or placement upon returning to their local school.

Personnel. An organization like CTY needs to recruit a strong leadership cadre. Because of the need for persons with both a strong liberal arts background and a knowledge of various levels of education (precollegiate and collegiate), good staff members are not easily found. Again, the organization confronts elements of the shadow politic of education. School persons are often suspected of lacking a comprehensive knowledge of a liberal arts discipline and a familiarity with university practice. Conversely, liberal arts students at the graduate level or young professors may consider the essentially precollegiate focus on CTY beneath their dignity as potential scholars. Regrettably, both viewpoints currently restrict the availability of a comprehensive CTY leadership cadre. It may be necessary therefore, to create that cadre through special degree programs at the university or through special teacher training activities for personnel from the precollegiate school system.

Quality Control. As CTY programs proliferate throughout the nation and abroad, there is a constant tension between those who recognize the need to adhere to the highest standards for both student identification and the academic programs and those who want the program to be more broadly accessible. Maintenance of quality control must remain a paramount responsibility requiring comprehensive methods of teacher orientation and training as well as careful review and evaluation procedures by the CTY main office in Baltimore. But that responsibility for quality control will continue to produce conflict with those persons who want to do everything for everyone in the name of non-elitism.

Recommendations and Warnings

School-college collaboration is a seemingly attractive way for attending to some of the inadequacies and inconsistencies of the American educational system. However, those schools and colleges that wish to engage in this practice must not be naive. If partnership is to be more than an easy, insubstantial gesture; if collaboration is to be more than another method of preserving the educational status quo, at two levels of education rather than one; if what is sought is a true partnership in which the peculiarities and definitions of each level of instruction are examined, evaluated, and adjusted; if the progress and well-being of the child are to be placed in the foreground, and not the self-interested preservation of the system; then school-college partnership must confront directly the shadow politic of education. Suspicions, prejudices, and assumptions developed over centuries which separate the various levels of educational institutions must be confronted and addressed. School-college collaboration can involve periods of tough in-fighting both between and among school educators and college educators. Partnerships that survive will be those that recognize the complexity of the effort, try not to please everyone, persist, and keep in mind the real focus of the effort—the well-being of the young people involved.

References

Benbow, C. P., and Stanley, J. C. (eds.). *Academic Precocity.* Baltimore, Md.: The Johns Hopkins University Press, 1976.

Durden, W. G. "The Johns Hopkins University Center for the Advancement of Academically Talented Youth: Its Place in American Education." In R. Sawyer, (ed.), *Meeting the Challenge,* Chapel Hill, N.C.: Duke University Press, forthcoming.

George, W. C., and others (eds.). *Educating the Gifted: Acceleration and Enrichment.* Baltimore, Md.: The Johns Hopkins University Press, 1979.

Stanley, J. C., and others (eds.). *Mathematical Talent: Discovery, Description, and Development.* Baltimore, Md.: The Johns Hopkins University Press, 1974.

William G. Durden is director of the Center for the Advancement of Academically Talented Youth and assistant professor of German at The Johns Hopkins University, Baltimore, Maryland. He has taught students from kindergarten through graduate school and is the author of numerous articles, books, and book reviews.

*The Middle College High School demonstrates what
can be done even for high risk students by a full
integration of high school, college, and the world of
work.*

Combining High School
and College:
LaGuardia's Middle College
High School

Janet E. Lieberman

The good news is: Educators who are dedicated to high school-college collaboration can replicate a "Middle College." The bad news is: Those same educators must allow two years preparation time and raise $50,000 for a planning, not an operational, budget. Given those two conditions, a workable institution can be built and will probably succeed.

For innovators, it is encouraging to remember that collaboration has been a feature of the scene since Eliot's Committee of Ten in 1886. Hutchins's pioneering venture at the University of Chicago in 1936 established the concepts of early admissions and advanced placement—programs that now accommodate more than 40,000 students annually. As a response to the recent critical national studies, administrators are looking closely at models of collaboratives. New structures may offer solutions to such familiar educational problems as declining enrollment, rising overhead costs, high attrition, underprepared students, and faculty burn out.

W. T. Daly. *College-School Collaboration: Appraising the Major Approaches.* New Directions for
Teaching and Learning, no. 24. San Francisco: Jossey-Bass, December 1985.

48

Origin

One model that addresses these issues is the Middle College, a high school program located on the LaGuardia Community College campus. Developed to solve some of the academic problems that the City University of New York faced in dealing with its underprepared students, the Middle College is a new substructure emphasizing the "seamless web of education" (Boyer, 1983). We began the planning in 1972, funded by the Carnegie Corporation and the Fund for the Improvement of Postsecondary Education. The intent was to design a school to reduce the dropout rate in urban high schools, to prepare students more effectively for work or college, and to attract more students to higher education. A major obstacle in working out the collaboration was centralizing the flow of money, as funding for high schools and colleges is traditionally separated. To overcome those administrative problems and to guarantee financial support, the school became a joint responsibility of the Board of Education and the Board of Higher Education of New York City, an unusual cooperative effort. The joint fiscal responsibility was crucial to institutionalizing reforms, as it guaranteed continued support and mutual interaction. Most collaboratives begin on soft money but they must eventually achieve municipal funding or wither and die. Having solved that and other problems up front, the school opened in 1974 with 125 students in the tenth grade. Each year 125 more tenth-grade students were added. The current enrollment is approximately 450 students, and covers the tenth, eleventh, and twelfth grades.

As a public alternative high school on a college campus, the program creates a continuum between high school and college. The Middle College structure also features flexible pacing, broad curricular options, service-oriented career education with required internships for all students, and a college environment. The underlying education philosophy is based on the psychosocial truism that fifteen-year-olds (the tenth-grade students) have more in common with twenty-year-olds than with twelve-year-olds and should be allowed to make their own educational choices.

Students come to Middle College voluntarily and with parental permission after local junior high schools have identified them as probable dropouts. Seventy-eight percent of the student body is on public assistance. All of the students participate in a program of cooperative education, where they work on three internships in three years, spending a third of each academic year at work.

Fitting into the College: The Cooperative Education Program

One of the major goals in establishing the collaborative was to mirror, as much as possible, the population and program of the college for the high school student. We recruited from the same socioeconomic level and from the same geographic area as the college. Since the college's major focus is cooperative education for all students, that work program was integral to our planning. At the outset, it was difficult to convince local employers of the seriousness of our students, as the community shared the stereotypical attitude toward teenagers. In spite of this, our students have now achieved a tremendous reputation for service to senior citizens, day-care centers, and hospitals.

We have found that the internship program, patterned after the college's cooperative education sequence, develops motivation and ultimately a sense of self-worth—strong factors in keeping adolescents in school. A "co-op prep" program, based on curricular materials developed in cooperation with the college faculty, prepares students for meaningful off-site educational experiences. College-level internships are also available for selected Middle College students. Advanced standing credit in the college co-op program is provided for Middle College graduates who subsequently enroll at LaGuardia.

General Curriculum and Organization

Students with deficiencies in basic skills participate in part-time internships, receiving remedial instruction in the early morning before going to their internship site. To fit into this cooperative education pattern, classes typically taught in sequential fashion have been redesigned along thematically coherent patterns. For example, American Studies, a year-long course that had been taught with a chronological approach, has been refashioned into three distinct, nonsequential, classes. The new courses, "Government and the Constitution," "Cultural Pluralism," and "American Foreign Policy," can be taken in any sequence, smoothing the way for the student who will be interrupting formal academic study with experiential learning.

In order to facilitate individual attention and to cope with significant skills deficits, Middle College classes are smaller than those typically found in urban high schools. Regular classes have maximum enrollment of twenty-seven students, and remedial classes have a limit of fifteen students per class. Each Middle College student spends three years (tenth, eleventh, and twelfth grades) in the school, with each year divided into three trimesters or cycles. Students qualify for a high school diploma when they complete the New York State requirements. Time needed to achieve that varies with student capabilities.

After the tenth grade, students have the opportunity, with permission of their counselors, to enroll in college courses. Scheduling is on an individual basis. The Middle College student takes these regular college courses with the community college students. These courses are free, part of their high school program, and the credit is also banked for their college requirements. Some Middle College students can amass as much as a year's college credit while still in high school. That opportunity reduces the amount of time required to obtain the associate (AA) degree. Implementing such a concept of continuity necessarily means individualizing the programming. Some students need more time than others. This combined curriculum gives students a broad range of choices. They make those choices with guidance from a faculty counselor to ensure that they meet the necessary requirements for both secondary school graduation and college entrance.

Problems and Solutions

Funding. One of the first major problems was establishing a funding pattern. The Middle College organizers tried many routes to have the money for high school students come through the municipality to the university so that there would be a unified budget. The mechanisms for doing that were not available, and the resultant compromise turned out surprisingly well. The high school division pays for the staff and usual per-pupil expenditures; the college provides the physical facilities.

Stereotypes. Another intangible problem results from the societal attitude towards teenagers as a sub-culture. At the outset of the project, Middle College students were blamed for every problem encountered by the institution. When the sprinkler system went off accidentally, it was the high school students' fault. Gradually, the principals worked with the security and maintenance staff to educate them and make them allies in our mission. Now the head of security, a former policeman, is an adjunct instructor teaching law and justice in Middle College, for high school credit.

Two Cultures. To make a "mesh" of high school and college programs, administrators need to recognize that the two educational settings represent distinct cultures. The contrasts in teacher preparation and in faculty attitudes at the secondary and postsecondary level dramatically define the separate cultures. As far as preparation is concerned, high school teachers usually graduate from schools of education where they take courses in methodology, in materials, and in psychology. They have limited concentration in their major discipline. That subject is frequently their major in college, but their programs usually include practice teaching and supervision, with a clear emphasis on education. College faculty, on the other hand, either have masters' or doctoral degrees in specific disciplines. They are experts in history, biology, or literature, but there is no preparation for college teaching. They have no courses in education and little knowledge of evaluation. Many have a love for their subject but not much experience teaching in the classroom or by means of any method other than lecture. That difference in training results in widely different classroom behaviors at the two levels of the system.

College instructors use the graduate school model—teaching as they have been taught, as discipline specialists. They offer the learning on a take-it-or-leave-it basis. The burden of learning is on the student. The college population is free to come or go, to learn or to fail. The reality is that the student who fails often leaves, but the professor feels no sense of inadequacy as a result. The high school teacher, in contrast, has a captive population, compelled to attend. The students remain, whether they pass or not. The teacher accepts full responsibility for having the students learn; there are few options on either side of the desk. If the student does not learn, the teacher experiences a sense of failure, and the system often condemns both the student and the teacher to repeat the experience. It is no wonder that a feeling of frustration charges the classrooms where this has occurred.

The separate cultures even have different titles, and with issues of titles come issues of status. The academic community has many curious ways of dividing the worlds of the college professor and that of the high school teacher. The values, environments, and resources are distinct. Pay scales do not match; work hours, schedules, responsibilities, all vary greatly. Unions differ, and with that come variations in licensing, hiring, tenure, and promotions. Credits, requirements, calendars are all incompatible. Achieving congruence between these two settings, along with subsequent continuity in the educational scheme requires elaborate bureaucratic maneuvers and sustained negotiations.

Counseling. Despite the differences in teacher preparation and in status, both faculties have one thing in common: neither has any required preparation in counseling techniques. In fact, as we began to assemble students and teachers, we found that our population's single most important need—a combined teacher-counselor—did not exist on any personnel roster. Our experience suggested that urban adolescents relate more effectively to a teacher who can also function as a counselor. Since the students' personal and educational problems are so closely meshed and their lives so fragmented, they need one individual and principal mentor who can work with them holistically.

To meet this need, Middle College originally created the position of teacher-counselor. The job description included functioning as a faculty counselor for a limited number of students in a new institutional unit, called the "house." The teacher and his or her advisees form the house group, which meets to discuss personal as well as school problems, social issues, and community activities. The result has been closer student-faculty relationships and clearer lines of responsibility.

By creating the new role of teacher-counselor, Middle College has to some degree changed the teachers' images of themselves. As teacher-counselors, the faculty members take initiative in obtaining community or parental support for the student. The teachers also seem to recognize more clearly their roles as academic models. It becomes part of their job. Every faculty member evaluates the students' achievement, and a discussion of that evaluation takes place with the house adviser in a joint conference with the student. Together the students and faculty consider curriculum and career choices. All this became possible when administrators redesigned the work week and replaced anachronistic custodial duties with work-load credit for working with students.

Professional Pride. In general, the separate worlds of college and high school faculty have resulted in a different sense of status for each group. College teachers usually remain aloof from high school problems or students. Their attitudes reflect the current structural separation, and they enjoy more public respect. High school teachers, suffering from difficult classroom conditions and a derogated self-image sadly reinforced by the system, often resent college personnel suggesting improvements. Each level often blames the other for its own failures. Many educational articulation experiments have failed because the innovators are insensitive to the distance between these separate worlds. Placing the high school on the college campus overcomes the status problem and creates a range of opportunities for both faculties.

Middle College teachers work as adjuncts in the college, a decided attraction because of the considerable increase in status. College faculty also teach at the high school giving them greater appreciation for their colleagues' problems. Aside from providing some financial rewards, both faculties gain additional stimulation in their professions. On one side, exposure to college students and to college faculty gives high school teachers a sense of what the college expects and provides a basis for continuity in curriculum planning. From the other side, college faculty have an opportunity to see the level of preparation of the students, and they can gauge their own teaching more realistically.

Economies. The faculties and the students at both levels share common facilities and have opportunities for informal exchange. This interchange has generated economies for the student and the institution. Five-year curricula, joint programs in career education, peer counseling, and college internships have been developed. Students escape the plague of "senioritis," and the programs do not repeat the senior year material in the freshman year of college. Much of this has required resolving some bureaucratic incompatibilities. Administrators have devised ratios reconciling high school work weeks and the classroom-contact-hour systems, thus allowing for more teacher exchange. The high school now uses the same class schedule—a quarter system—as the college, and shares the gym, the lounges, the labs, the library, and the cafeterias. After ten years, compatibility is virtually complete.

Discipline. At the Middle College, both the college classrooms and high school classrooms have benefited from the power of a shared site. The usually large, compulsory high school setting frequently contains many rules and more punishments for infractions. In most urban settings, restriction and frustration have resulted in aggression. In the college, however, with the same population, there are fewer incidents of violence.

College students exist in a voluntary setting. They are free to cut some classes and to make choices among an array of options. Middle College founders recognized this major difference in the freedom of the environments was significant in helping the adolescent make a smoother transition from high school to college. The educational setting was formed to encourage the adolescent to learn to handle freedom, to make his or her own decisions, and to take responsibility for those decisions. As in college, high school students working with an adviser choose their courses and their career exploration. They are treated as college students, free to leave the building, to go out for lunch, to smoke, to hang out, but they know the realistic consequences if they abuse this freedom.

The assumption of adulthood and respect for personal decisions may be a key to the success of Middle College. The students repeatedly cite freedom as the quality they like best about the school. Discipline problems are rare, and students quickly learn the mores of the institution. Treating the adolescents as adults may also address the drop-out problem, because it gives them a taste of future possibilities and hence induces some long-term planning. It is a significant factor in leading them toward higher education—in contrast to the terminal atmosphere of most high schools.

When asked, students frequently complain about the "unreality" of the ordinary high school classroom. At LaGuardia, we have tried to overcome that isolation with the previously described program of career exploration and education for all students. Within that context, students recognize that they have choices and some control over their destinies. Awareness of options and a sense of control are important determinants for minority students. The continuity of career education becomes a realistic thread, reducing the student tendency to view school as unrelated to life.

Finally, holding high school classes in a college setting provides an atmosphere where secondary students subtly modify their behavior to be accepted by the college population. The college environment not only penetrates the insularity of the teenage culture but also encourages the adolescents to take advantage of the prerogative of adult status. They commingle with college students, and they respond maturely. The peer model of the college student enables them to see themselves two years later; they recognize that they too can succeed. The feedback in motivation is obvious. Middle College students carry a college ID; they use the bookstore; they work out in the gym. That participation in college life has a

54

positive impact on the adolescents' self-image. Their value system changes, and education becomes more appealing. The Student Services division of the college has institutionalized this change in self-image by training college students to do peer counseling of high school students in groups. High school students then learn peer counseling techniques and work with their own age group. This experience has been a very successful one. It promotes understanding and tolerance and leads to self-governance.

The student population contains a wide range of ethnic minorities, but perhaps because of the factors just discussed, the Middle College, in ten years of existence, has not had any of the racial conflict so characteristic of urban schools.

Evidence of Success

The positive reaction of students and teachers to the Middle College is clear from the long waiting list we have of students wanting to come to Middle College, and from the stability of the instructional staff. The Middle College has no trouble retaining staff. That may be partly because of small class sizes. It is also because of job satisfaction and the college connection.

But the real measure of any educational institution is the performance of its students. And, for Middle College's student clientele, academic success is not a foregone conclusion. Middle College has undertaken to educate a population that is not the "cream" of good students off the top of the high school classes. Indeed, students are recruits for the program beause they have been identified as potential dropouts. And yet, the Middle College has an attrition rate of 14.5 percent compared to the New York City-wide published average of 46 percent (which includes the gifted). The average attendance is 84.5 percent, also higher than the city average. In spite of the high-risk population, more than 90 percent of the senior class graduates, and more than 85 percent of those graduates go on to higher education. (About 50 percent of the latter group go to LaGuardia.)

In short, the creation of Middle College accomplished major changes with minor upheavals. By designing a new structure, the college was able to overcome many traditional problems and to respond more effectively to students' developmental needs. We believe the core of our model is replicable. Variations of it already exist in other urban areas. Attempts at a repeat performance will, of course, require tailoring to specific needs; but, in general, articulation efforts such as this one can offer positive and productive educational experiences for everyone: the students, the administrators, and the faculty.

Reflections and Recommendations

Time. The first suggestion for educators who are considering major institutional innovations such as the Middle College, is to define goals carefully and to develop programs consistent with these goals. To do this, a year of planning is needed and a minimum of $50,000. Do not let administrative pressure push you into a premature start.

Second, the partnerships must have cooperation at the highest level of administration from both the high school and the college sector—superintendent to chancellor. Programs that begin counselor-to-counselor or faculty-to-faculty have trouble making it. Similarly, the community, and the teachers, need time to understand the new structure and to accept its nontraditional approach. Although cooperation at the top is necessary, some projects fail because they have not included all participants in the planning. High school personnel, in particular, need full partnership in the project design. Such dialogue helps to provide a feeling of participation and replaces the ever-present paranoia with a sense of trust.

Time is also necessary to bridge the two cultures of high school and college faculty and to institutionalize the new structure. The institution needs ample opportunity to develop strategies that enable faculty to cross the educational levels and to arrange approvals for credit banking.

Incentives. Both levels of faculty need incentives to teach beyond their assigned students. The plan should include appropriate rewards for both groups. From the college viewpoint, for example, working with the high school should count for tenure and promotion or time off—incentives that are real and germane.

One way to provide incentives for administrative personnel is to anchor the high school personnel in the college framework. For example, the director of the high school portion of the program might be made part of the college administration by giving him or her a position equal to a college chairperson. Otherwise, liaison persons appointed by the college usually twist painfully in the wind. Faculty acting in a liaison capacity operate on the fringe of both high school and college. They have no decision-making powers in either setting and, consequently, merely convey messages. Not being firmly rooted in either institution, they may even be bypassed in routine communications. Because they do not have the necessary institutional authority, liaisons can only persuade and cajole. To succeed, the institutions need to give the collaborative a position of priority, one where it will have a voice in the operational framework.

Facilities. Ideally, collaboratives should share physical facilities. This creates the optimal environment for students to learn from each other. The example of peers who have made it, and the informal mentoring that occurs in a shared physical environment is invaluable for motivation and support.

To work effectively, the innovative collaborative also demands a cheerful physical setting. The buildings housing the program should not be the ones no one else wants, or those long decayed by disuse. Try not to ghettoize the program.

Curriculum. Planning a self-paced curriculum involves working out the relations of competency, mastery, and evaluation. It also involves making the high school and college match in classroom periods and yearly schedules. All aspects of curricular collaboration will work better if the number of students is small. Fewer than 500 students is desirable. Finally, viewing the high school-college sequence as an eight year span provides more options for teaching desired skills and content. Given eight years time, particularly in light of the current overlap between the senior year in high school and the freshman year in college, we can design new, more effective sequences in virtually every subject area.

Similar options are also available using another combination, namely, combining the last two years of high school, the two community college years and the last two years at a senior college (2+2+2). The Ford Foundation is currently encouraging such articulation and transfer proposals between community and senior colleges in a nationwide program intended for urban, minority students.

Efforts like the Ford Foundation's reflect a readiness for change in the educational world. There is a chance for everyone to get into the act: teacher organizations, state agencies, local schools, and individual educators. In the future, we will undoubtedly see new types of educational collaboratives, encompassing the high school and the college years, and perhaps even professional training. The sequence is likely to vary from public to private setting, and for pupils of different levels of ability. But it will almost surely involve closer cooperation among the various levels of education in pursuit of flexibility in and sharing of institutional resources. Sharing that will be necessary to broaden the pool of students upon which higher education can draw, and to adapt to the diversity of that student pool.

References

Boyer, E. L. *High School: A Report on Secondary Education in America.* New York: Harper & Row, 1983.

Ravitch, D. "Seminars on Innovations in Education," (presentation) Columbia University, 1985.

Janet E. Lieberman, a professor of psychology at LaGuardia Community College of the City University of New York, is the founder and originator of the Middle College High School at LaGuardia. A developmental psychologist with more than twenty-five years experience in the New York City schools, she is currently co-director of the Ford Foundation's Urban Community College Transfer Opportunities Program, and director of The Council of Articulated Programs.

PART 3.

Working with Teachers

With 138 sites nationwide and over 70,000 teachers participating each year, the National Writing Project offers an existing and readily available opportunity for affiliation in pursuit of improved writing instruction.

Joining a National Network: The National Writing Project

James Gray

When we planned the Bay Area Writing Project in the early 1970s, most teachers—no matter at what grade level they taught: elementary, secondary, or college—were not trained to teach writing. The second 'R' had been ignored for reasons that are still difficult to identify. Writing was taken for granted. Elementary teachers were trained to teach reading, and secondary teachers—if they were English majors—were trained in the history of English literature. In the other disciplines there was little if any attention to the fundamental role writing can have in aiding student learning. When we asked teachers, "What university or what university course taught you to teach writing?" they seldom had an answer. Although more was becoming known about writing and the teaching of writing than ever before, most teachers—working as they do in the islands of their own classrooms—were generally uninformed, with no systematic way of becoming informed. There was another problem. Teachers, particularly secondary teachers, were increasingly cynical about mandated in-service programs that seldom focused on the subject matter of teaching; programs conducted by outside consultants—"take-the-money-and-run" consultants—who all too frequently had no classroom teaching experience.

W. T. Daly. *College-School Collaboration: Appraising the Major Approaches.* New Directions for Teaching and Learning, no. 24. San Francisco: Jossey-Bass, December 1985.

62

It was also in the early 1970s, however, that universities were beginning to report sharp increases in the number of entering freshmen who were required to take a remedial writing course before being admitted to the regular freshman English sequence. Writing is the most difficult of all language acts. At the University of California–Berkeley there had always been a sizable number of freshmen required to take the university's Subject A course, even though these students had graduated in the top 12.5 percent of their high school classes. But by 1973 that number had alarmingly increased to over 40 percent.

Something had to be done, and all of the schools had to be involved in the solution, for writing is a skill that needs constant repetition and attention at every level. It was clear that the universities alone could not solve the writing problem. However, we needed a new model of university-school collaboration, for past university efforts to improve the schools had been heavily "top-down" in design; and this design had proved ineffective. Whatever we were going to do, we wanted to do it right—not repeat what we had come to see as the flaws in past programs. Project English, for example, had generated scores of excellent materials in the mid-to-late-1960s that for the most part went unread. The earlier NDEA English Institutes were highly regarded by teachers, but as carefully screened and selected as the NDEA teachers were, once they were in residence their expertise was seldom tapped. Teachers were students taking more course work in these university programs, and were treated, in effect, as undergraduates. And there were no follow-up programs, no plans to keep teachers working together over time, no plans to have the teachers who attended the institutes work with other teachers.

We not only wanted to design a program that would more effectively extend teacher knowledge; we also wanted to recognize what successful teachers had already learned about the teaching of writing out of their own trial and error classroom experiences. While most teachers were ill-trained to teach writing, there were some teachers who had developed (often as a result of their own personal interest in writing) their own successful approaches. We knew there were many teachers who did know what they were doing when they taught writing and why they were doing it. We wanted to put these informed teachers to work teaching others. We wanted a model that would celebrate good teaching and good teachers, a model that would put a premium on what was actually working in the classroom.

The National Writing Project

Objectives. The writing project we established in response to these needs, first in the Bay Area and then nationally, had four major objectives: (1) to improve student writing by improving the teaching of writing; (2) to provide an effective staff development model for the schools; (3) to provide an effective model for university-school collaboration; and (4) to extend the professional roles of classroom teachers.

The Basic Model. Essentially a staff-development program, the National Writing Project is based on the belief that the key agent in educational change is the teacher. As a first step, therefore, National Writing Project site directors identify master teachers of writing in their geographical areas from all levels of instruction, elementary school through university. They then bring these master teachers together on university campuses for intensive five-week-long summer institutes that focus on three closely interrelated activities: demonstration by teachers of their most successful classroom practices; study of current theory and research in the teaching of composition; and practice in writing in a variety of forms—personal, literary, persuasive, and expository. The aims of the institute are simple: to provide teachers a setting in which they can share classroom successes; to help them broaden and make more conscious the grounds of their teaching; to give teachers an opportunity to commit themselves intensely and reflectively to the process of writing; and, finally, to identify a corps of master classroom teachers who can effectively teach the techniques and processes of teaching writing to other teachers. Through this process—which continues with regular meetings throughout the school year—these exemplary classroom teachers are trained as a corps of writing project teacher-consultants. The most qualified teacher-consultants, in turn, conduct the school-year in-service programs that the writing project sponsors in the surrounding schools and districts. Annually, some 3,000 classroom teachers now participate in this summer institute training, and approximately 70,000 teachers participate in the range of summer and school-year programs offered by the network of writing project sites.

The Network. Over the past twelve years, the National Writing Project has expanded into a national network of local university-school writing projects—each based on the staff development model and program design of the initial Bay Area Writing Project, described above, which continues to serve as the lead administrative agency. Currently, the national network numbers 138 sites, 121 in the United States (in 44 states), 4 serving American teachers teaching overseas in American independent and dependent schools, and 6 international sites located in Canada, England, Australia, Sweden, and Finland. Fourteen universities in the United States are now planning new sites for 1986 start-up dates, and a new site is now being planned in Norway. The goal of the National Writing Project is to extend this network so that teachers in all states and in all regions of the country can be served by a local writing project site; approximately 250 sites nationwide will be needed to meet this goal.

The Basic Assumptions. While each site in the network is autonomous and designed to serve its own geographic region, all National Writing

64

Project sites are recognizably similar, follow the same teacher-teaching-teacher model, and base their programs on the same set of key assumptions:

1. Since the writing problem affects both the universities and the schools, it can best be solved through cooperatively planned university-school programs.

2. Student writing can be improved by improving the teaching of writing, and the best teacher of teachers is another teacher.

3. Successful teachers of writing can be identified, brought together during university summer institutes, and trained to teach other teachers in follow-up programs in the schools.

4. What is known about the teaching of writing comes not only from research but from the practice of those who teach writing.

5. Programs designed to improve the teaching of writing should involve teachers at all grade levels and from all subject areas.

6. Change can best be accomplished by those who work in the schools, and not by transient consultants nor by packets of teacher-proof materials.

7. Change in classroom practice happens over time, through staff development programs that are on-going and systematic.

8. The intuition of teachers can be a productive guide for field-based research, and practicing teachers can conduct useful studies in their own classrooms.

9. Teachers of writing must write themselves.

Funding. Since 1976–77, the Bay Area Writing Project has provided modest matching grants to new National Writing Project sites with funds provided by the National Endowment for the Humanities and, more recently, by the Andrew W. Mellon Foundation. Current funding for this purpose runs through 1985–86, and we are now conducting a major fund-raising campaign to secure new sources of support. Many sites, however, have been funded entirely through local funds, particularly in those states that have secured legislative support for the development of statewide networks of writing project sites. Six states now provide some measure of state support: California Writing Project (19 sites), Virginia Writing Project (10 sites), and the single statewide sites serving Alaska and Hawaii.

Affiliation with the National Writing Project

Affiliation with the National Writing Project begins with a request for New Site Guidelines. It involves securing support from the host college, involving interested schools in the planning, securing local funding (some matching funds from the national project may be available), and a two- to three-day planning meeting conducted by personnel from the central Berkeley office.

Affiliation brings to the new site all of the benefits of belonging to an established and recognized project with its own active network, a network that is both formal and informal. Local site directors remain in close contact with the lead agency at U.C.-Berkeley, but they also establish close professional and personal ties with one another, particularly in those states with multiple sites. It is the networking that gives this national project identity and coherence and keeps it from being merely a collection of isolated sites. The lead agency publishes the *National Writing Project Network Newsletter,* a quarterly publication to which local sites contribute, as well as four publication series written by National Writing Project Teacher/Consultants: (1) curriculum and teacher-research monographs; (2) the National Writing Project Writing Teacher-At-Work series; (3) a series that presents in detail the classroom work of exemplary teachers; and (4) a set of occasional papers. The lead agency also publishes a portfolio of evaluation studies conducted at local National Writing Project sites that document the impact the project has had on improved student writing and the teaching of writing. An annual National Writing Project Directors Meeting is held each fall preceding the annual convention of the National Council of Teachers of English, and an annual retreat for the continuing education of site directors is held each spring at Wildacres in North Carolina. Each year the Bay Area Writing Project receives detailed reports from each local National Writing Project site and, with the data and information provided, publishes its own annual report of the National Writing Project. Key highlight sections of this compiled report are then distributed to all sites. A National Writing Project Advisory Board of site directors representing different regions of the country meets twice each year to advise the lead agency staff on matters of policy.

Keys to a Successful Site

The National Writing Project is a flexible and open program, and new sites, once they have been approved, are completely autonomous. But the local sites of the National Writing Project also have a common purpose and an identifiable integrity based on their common acceptance and belief in the project's basic assumptions and program model. While refinement of the Bay Area Writing Project model is constant and encouraged, any major swings away from the spirit of that model, any outright dismissal of a key component, or even any half-hearted or token compliance with some important aspect of that model could weaken considerably a local site and, by implication, the whole national network. The key components of the model are discussed below.

The Selection Process. The selection of the best possible teachers for the invitational summer institutes is crucial! The summer institute is not meant to assist teachers in need of help. The success of the institute and all subsequent writing project programs depends upon the careful identification of demonstrably effective teachers, teachers who are both strong and open, teachers with the potential of being as effective with fellow teachers as they have been with their own students. As a result, we recommend an initial nomination procedure rather than an open application program, with the final selection determined by personal interviews with the most promising candidates.

Teacher Demonstrations. When we invite successful teachers to demonstrate and discuss their own best practices, we are tapping what successful teachers know: that particular and real knowledge of how to teach writing that comes *only* from the practice of teaching writing. That we spend so much time during the institutes focusing on teacher knowledge has an enormous impact. When teachers are respected, when they are treated not as empty vessels to be filled but as the experts they are, they gain in strength, they become less defensive and more open. Such an atmosphere breeds trust, and teachers from the universities and the schools can begin to work together as respected colleagues interested in what both worlds have to offer.

Teachers need sufficient time to conduct these "trial-run" in-service workshops during the institute. At the Bay Area Writing Project we schedule two such workshops during each three-and-a-half-hour morning session, with each teacher demonstration discussed and evaluated not only for content but for effectiveness of presentation.

The Focus on Writing. As classroom teachers begin writing again, as they make time in the summer to write, rewrite, and reflect upon their own writing and have the opportunity to discuss their own written pieces with others who are also writing, they gain an understanding about writing and the writing process and a new understanding about the teaching of writing they would not have had simply through the examination of best practices, or through discussion, or through reading and study alone.

Three afternoons each week the teachers meet in small editing and response groups to discuss and edit the major writing assignments they have been asked to do outside of class. At the Bay Area Writing Project, teachers write four such pieces ranging from personal memoirs to essays to personal position papers on the teaching of writing. Each teacher's best piece is published in an annual anthology. Teachers are frequently asked to write during the teaching demonstrations in the morning sessions. This emphasis on teachers' writing is continued during the in-service sessions of the school site programs.

For many teachers, this strong focus on their own writing has been the most valuable component of the summer institute. It is the writing that brings the program full circle.

The Focus on Research. The summer institute is an opportunity to wed the two worlds of knowledge and practice: in weekly seminars on research findings on such themes as the process of writing, response to student writing, revision, writing across the curriculum; in teacher demonstrations that refer to supporting research; and in the project's focus on teacher research. When teachers, for example, begin to think of themselves as potential researchers and begin to design their own classroom-research studies, the writing project—in a very easy and natural way—opens up teacher interest in the research that already exists.

Follow-up Programs for Teachers. When we invite teachers to the summer institute we tell them that they are in for the duration, that the writing project can become a career-long commitment. The writing project does become an on-going support group for teachers, a new professional organization that keeps teachers tied together through its working corps of teacher-consultants, its frequent Saturday morning meetings, its publication and teacher research programs, its advisory teacher councils and executive committees, and its target groups that keep teachers working together around topics of common interest. Through these follow-up programs, teacher involvement with the writing project continues long after the summer institute is over.

School Year School Site Programs. While the summer institute is the central program of the writing project, the key program out of which everything else springs, the project has its greatest impact and trains the greatest number of teachers in the school-year programs. That so many teachers have responded to these school-year programs is testimony to the National Writing Project's key assumption that successful, full-time, practicing teachers are the most effective teachers of other teachers and have a credibility that no other consultants can match. The basic Bay Area Writing Project school in-service model has the following features:

• A series of ten sessions planned in consultation with school-district teachers and administrators. No single-shot sessions. Three-hour sessions so that teachers will have time to examine specific approaches and time to try out these ideas in their own writing. A full-year effort that can be continued year after year.

• Workshops conducted by trained, full-time practicing teachers, with a coordinator present at all sessions to guarantee the coherence and integrity of the program.

• Workshops scheduled after school hours and open to all teachers who wish to attend. Because of the National Writing Project policy not to conduct mandated in-service programs, National Writing Project teacher-consultants know that those teachers who attend these workshops are present because they want to be and are eager to learn. In such an atmosphere, in-service programs are usually successful, and because of the positive response of those teachers who attend the first year, the teachers who stayed away are frequently drawn into the program in year two or year three.

Open Stance. The National Writing Project is a program that is open to whatever is known about the teaching of writing from whatever source, from the literature in the field, from research, and from the insights and experiences of successful teachers. The writing project has no packaged plans, no teacher-proof materials, no set formulas for the teaching of writing. We promote no single approach to the teaching of writing, even though we recognize a number of ideas that have emerged over the past decade and are now being adopted by an increasing number of teachers. The National Writing Project remains open to discovery and open to qualification, and this position is the sustaining strength of the project.

Evaluation

In 1970 the Carnegie Corporation of New York funded a three-year, outside evaluation of the writing project that was completed with nineteen technical reports. In his executive summary, Michael Scriven, evaluation director, stated that the writing project "appears to be the best large-scale effort to improve composition instruction now in operation in this country, and certainly is the best on which substantial data are available." In 1983, the Bay Area Writing Project published the *National Writing Project Evaluation Portfolio,* a collection of thirty-two evaluation studies conducted at National Writing Project sites nationwide. This portfolio includes positive data on: impact on student writing; impact on teacher attitudes and practices; and impact on administrators, on program costs, and on professional activities of teachers. The thirty-two studies included from the more than sixty available were those that: satisfied the requirements of evaluation designs; had data available for analysis; had completed all stages of the study; and had available written reports of the results.

James Gray is a senior lecturer at the University of California-Berkeley's School of Education. He is the founder and director of the Bay Area Writing Project and the National Writing Project.

With over 100 groups in 40 states, the Academic Alliances Program offers an existing opportunity for affiliation with a collaborative designed to bring together teachers, from all levels of the educational system, as professionals concerned with the quality of education in their respective disciplines.

Local Communities of Inquiry: Penn's Academic Alliances Program

Claire Gaudiani

Two paradoxes currently at work in American education are driving some of the best teaching minds out of the nation's schools and into other careers.

Paradox No. 1

Those who spend the most time developing our children's minds are not encouraged to develop their own. Americans do not value the intellectual ability of school teachers. Our school systems make them go begging for status in the community, for time and incentive to keep up with their subject, and for opportunities to develop new academic interests and expand old ones.

Paradox No. 2

We do value the intellectual ability of our college faculty, yet we encourage their isolation and segregation from school teachers. Universities and the academic community encourage continuing scholarly

W. T. Daly. *College-School Collaboration: Appraising the Major Approaches.* New Directions for Teaching and Learning, no. 24. San Francisco: Jossey-Bass, December 1985.

study and specialization among professors, requiring of them on average only nine to fourteen hours of class per week and often giving them special support and time for research and attendance at conferences. College faculty are not, however, expected to share this knowledge on a regular basis with school teachers who teach classes in the very same subject in the very same town. College faculty who treat school teachers as professional colleagues are committing what could be considered an unnatural act.

Academic Alliances

In the past four years in 40 states and the Virgin Islands, more than 2,000 faculty members in schools and colleges are resolving these two paradoxes. These faculty members now meet together regularly as professional colleagues. At their monthly or bi-monthly meetings in their local communities they keep each other up-to-date in the subjects they are teaching. They share publications and research findings, design and cooperate on interinstitutional learning projects, and stimulate and challenge each other intellectually. In short, they rediscover the pleasure and excitement of studying their disciplines with other adults committed to the academic life. More than 100 Academic Alliance groups now exist in foreign languages, English, history, biology, chemistry, and physics.

Models from Other Professions. Academic Alliances are modeled on the original conception of the county medical society and bar association. Each of the existing collaboratives draws together from fifteen to fifty faculty members from the schools and colleges in a local area, all of whom teach the same academic discipline. Whereas in-service education for teachers is typically planned by supervisors and administrators, Academic Alliance meetings, as are their legal and medical counterparts, are planned by teachers themselves who are committed to their own intellectual growth. Faculty members at all levels take responsibility for the quality of teaching and learning in their disciplines in their local areas and learn to rely on each other as primary sources of intellectual growth. The Academic Alliance project is built on the assumption that teachers, working collectively, can be a powerful and cost-effective force in improving the quality of their own professional lives.

Unifying the Profession. Members help each other maintain a spirit of inquiry crucial to the healthy intellectual life of all members regardless of the age of their students. Collaborative groups also allow faculty already established in their profession to serve as mentors to their younger colleagues. To this end, many alliance groups include college seniors and master's and doctoral degree candidates who are preparing for careers in teaching. Together, members focus on finding common ground, sharing common concerns, and working together toward common professional goals. Unlike most summer institutes and workshops, collaborative group meetings create on-going long-term, faithful, professional relationships among those who teach the same subjects in the same local area.

Thus, the philosophy underlying this project rejects the segregation of faculty in the schools from those who teach at the colleges and university levels. Regardless of the students they teach, kindergarten to graduate school, all faculty members need to continue learning in order to teach effectively. Faculty collaboratives work against the isolation that is a common complaint of classroom teachers. They help faculty members themselves to improve continuity in the curriculum. They also encourage teachers to appreciate highly developed specializations within a field while also focusing their attention on the broad shape of the discipline within the American curriculum.

Relations with Other Professional Organizations. The relationship of these local alliances to the existing regional and state teacher organizations has been an important issue in many areas. Groups have tended to thrive best where the relationship was clear and complementary. Ideally, collaborative groups meet monthly except during the months a state or regional meeting is scheduled. Between major, larger meetings, local faculty create on-going opportunities for themselves in the smaller, more focused collaboratives. They disseminate the information from the regional meetings and develop and shape future agendas through the professional work they do together in the more informal local settings. Teachers who have been long inactive in state and regional organizations can often become re-engaged through involvement in the local alliance groups. Thus, national, regional, and state organizations are likely to be strengthened by a more active, professionally engaged faculty at the local level.

What Happens at Meetings

At each meeting, the program itself helps build a community of scholars among those who teach a particular discipline. Meetings are often devoted to the following kinds of activities.

Journal Review. Colleagues help each other keep up-to-date in their discipline by preparing abstracts of important articles in the current literature in the field. At each meeting, several group members report on journal readings. The reports might concentrate on a single issue of a recent journal or on articles from several journals which address a common theme. Few faculty members subscribe to all the journals they should read; few have the time to read them thoroughly. As a result, faculty members can save each other time and build common intellectual interests through journal review at meetings.

Panel Discussions. These programs are designed to challenge teachers to think in new ways about their disciplines or to consider again central issues and texts of long-standing importance to those engaged in the discipline. In some collaboratives, colleagues select one or two areas of major concern to those in their field as a focus for the year's meetings. Each meeting then includes a special program on one of those concerns. Group members themselves plan and present this part of the meeting on a rotating basis. College faculty collaborate with—rather than dominate—their colleagues from other academic sectors. School teachers as well as professors present programs; in fact, many do so together with their colleagues from the college level.

Demonstration Classes and Curriculum Exchanges. In these meetings, colleagues help each other improve teaching in their discipline, since it is in the best interest of all teachers that their subjects be well taught. In some collaborative groups, teachers have found ways to improve articulation, share teaching resource materials, upgrade segments of the curriculum, and increase student interest in the subject area. Some teachers eventually feel confident enough to visit one another's classes and exchange testing and teaching techniques.

Reviews of Major Conferences of General Interest. Rising travel costs and shrinking departmental and system-wide budgets have caused great reductions in travel funds for many faculty. As a result, many teachers cannot afford to attend professional meetings. Those who do attend can quickly and efficiently disseminate information presented there upon returning to their collaborative groups. Thus, these groups complement the on-going work done at state, regional, and national meetings. Colleagues may also be able to assist each other in securing more opportunities to travel to discipline-specific conferences. Often, school teachers have the most limited opportunities. Postsecondary faculty can help make the case for travel funds to school boards.

What Does Not Happen at Meetings

Postsecondary faculty do *not* dominate school faculty or take sole responsibility for quality programming. Despite differences in levels of terminal degrees, teachers in the same discipline can and do find common ground and learn from and teach each other.

Outside experts do *not* dominate the agenda. Teachers learn to rely on each other to become the experts. Together faculty help each other refuse the passive role of spectator in the discipline and accept instead the active role of researcher and scholar.

A small clique does *not* exert a strangle hold on group's activities.

There are *no* lengthy lectures that cut off opportunities for questions or reduce the importance of preparatory outside reading by group members.

How Groups Get Started

Collaboratives are typically initiated by small core groups of interested faculty from schools and colleges who gradually identify others and build the alliance. Alliances typically have from twelve to sixty members. All alliances share a fundamental similarity critical to their success: Membership is open to faculty and administrators from all educational levels from university to elementary school in the same cities, counties, or regions, but only to those teaching or working in the same or closely related disciplines. Those interested in establishing an alliance might proceed as follows.

Step One: Identify Interested Faculty. Teachers in the schools or colleges may begin the process. Administrators may also initiate groups. In one state, the executive director of the State Humanities Council inspired faculty to develop local alliance groups. A faculty initiative might involve contacting faculty in one's own department and those in local area schools and colleges who teach your discipline, and asking them to announce to their colleagues your intent to form a faculty collaborative. The local board of education or the state coordinator may provide lists of elementary- and secondary-level faculty members. Contact those with a reputation for professional service and leadership.

An administrative initiative might involve contacting the department heads or selected faculty at your institution and encouraging them to establish a collaborative group in their own disciplines. With the help of department heads, invite administrators and faculty from other academic sectors and neighboring institutions to meet with you and your faculty. Together, the administrators and faculty should discuss the benefits of this project's collaborative mode of faculty development and realistic incentives for those who help establish or join collaboratives. If faculty express interest in forming a collaborative group, you might offer the stationery, stamps, telephone, and secretarial support that they will need to establish a group expeditiously.

Step Two: Establish a Steering Committee. Almost all collaborative groups need a steering committee in the early stages of development. The committee should include representatives of all possible educational levels offering a subject in the area. Postsecondary faculty members should not dominate the committee—either in number or in perceived importance. Those who specialize in pedagogy, as well as those who specialize in research, should serve on the committee. In forming steering committees, members of the existing collaboratives have suggested that you either select and persuade some of your most promising prospective members to serve, or ask for volunteers at a general meeting.

Step Three: Establish the Collaborative Groups. The steering committee should meet to make a founding statement which: defines the geographic area in which the collaborative group will operate; determines initial goals; states the major issues of concern to the local faculty in that discipline; and suggests specific incentives to encourage faculty participation in the group. Preparing this statement may require several meetings. At the final meeting, the steering committee should establish the date, time, and location of the first meeting of the entire collaborative group.

The committee should send copies of the statement to local administrators in the schools, community colleges, colleges, and universities, and ask that they nominate faculty to attend the first meeting. Steering committee members may decide to visit leading administrators and explain the objectives as well as institutional benefits of faculty collaboratives; for example: cost-effective in-service education and faculty development; a means of building enrollment through contact with high schools; inexpensive community outreach; and recognition as a leader in improving American education. The committee should secure a letter of endorsement for the collaborative group from each administrator.

The steering committee should then send its statement with a letter of invitation to prospective group members. The invitation should describe the concept of a collaborative group, the group's goals, and the major concerns to be addressed, and indicate the date, time, and place of the first meeting. A telephone call or written reminder one week prior to the first meeting will improve attendance. The reminder might include a copy of the agenda. The first meeting should occur at a centrally located site.

At the meeting, the steering committee should provide background information about this concept of collaboration and describe the proposed format of future meetings. (The Academic Alliance office has a videotape called "The Concept of Collaboration: Getting Off the Bus" which is available, together with consulting services, to help new groups understand and implement collegial faculty development.) The *entire group* should begin to decide which concerns it hopes to address at the local level. Members should also determine together the date, time, location, and agenda of the next meeting. Members will need to select a convenient meeting schedule. Some collaborative groups have arranged with local school systems for elementary and secondary faculty to have one-and-a-half hours of released time each month on the afternoon of their meeting. Finally, the members will need to elect officers. Often co-chairpersons head the group, one teacher from the schools and one from postsecondary levels sharing leadership roles.

Faculty will also need to consider how to expand the group's membership. Some collaboratives invite student teachers, graduate students, and majors to their meetings. In this way, these new colleagues make the transition from training to practice in a community of scholars in their discipline. Follow-up is also important. The committee should contact those who did not attend and invite them to the next meeting. Submitting an article about the initial meeting to the local newspaper(s) may lead to an increase in attendance at the next meeting.

Most teachers have negative responses to "another meeting." Collaborative meetings run *by* faculty *for* faculty are rare. Members will initially need to be convinced that they can help determine the program and that the program will be substantive and related to their subject areas and responsive to their needs and interests. Many teachers also expect postsecondary faculty to dominate meetings with school faculty. They will also need to be convinced that the group will treat all teachers as colleagues, each with valuable knowledge to receive and impart.

Incentive for Academic Alliances

The creation of incentives involves a change in the academic value system in many areas of the country. In some areas school teachers receive in-service, continuing education, or recertification credit. In others, teachers receive released time, comp time, or exemption from extracurricular activities for participation.

College and university faculty need to be given credit for their work with their university and school-level colleagues, perhaps under the "teaching" category rather than the less influential "service" category. In some colleges, work with the local Academic Alliances group counts as committee work and releases members from additional institutional service. Others have even provided some reduction in teaching load for those in leadership roles.

Changing the incentive and reward structure will require a long-term effort. Typically, faculty members and administratrors have helped each other to design appropriate incentives to encourage both school and college faculty to participate.

Funding

Academic Alliance groups are voluntary local organizations and they require relatively modest outside funding to maintain regular activities. Grant monies for start-up funding have, however, been available. The Academic Alliance model was originally launched in 1981 among foreign language faculty across the country through a project entitled "Strengthening the Humanities Through Foreign Language and Literature Studies." In the course of this project, funded by the National Endowment for the Humanities, the Rockefeller Foundation, the MacArthur Foundation and the Exxon Education Foundation, seventy-five groups of foreign language and literature faculty were established using the model.

Since 1983, the project has been expanded to cover the other academic disciplines taught in both schools and colleges across the country.

The American Historical Association has recently received start-up funds to launch History Alliances. Two foundations are preparing to support the launching of alliance groups in English, math, and the sciences. In each of the disciplines, grant funds support a central office and project director who develops and publicizes the project model among school and college faculty in the discipline. This is accomplished by arranging for publications in professional journals and newsletters, by conferences, and by contact with chief state school officers and state education supervisors, as well as by faculty addresses at state and national professional meetings of teachers of the discipline.

The operations of individual groups at the local level vary widely in the amount of funding they require. Four foreign language alliance groups, for example, received funding from the state humanities committee for summer institutes designed and taught by alliance members. Other groups received small amounts of funding from local foundations and still others received operations support fom school districts or the college or university where the alliance was based.

A number of the new groups have established community advisory boards that include business and community leaders. These groups can often advise on the availability of funds to support teachers' need for materials, travel, and guest speakers.

The National Endowment for the Humanities has recently launched a special program to fund projects by groups of school and college faculty working collaboratively in the same discipline. Information on this competition is available from the National Endowment for the Humanities, Washington, D.C.

Given the fact that four-year institutions whose faculty participate are likely to realize a student recruitment advantage, the central office at Academic Alliances has been able to make a persuasive argument that these institutions should make small amounts of funds available on a continuing basis to support the secretarial and office costs of maintaining a working alliances group.

Finally, several collaborative groups have discovered that federal, state, and local funding is found more easily and spread more widely if they can collaborate on their grant proposals.

Evaluation

While no formal evaluation of the impact of Academic Alliance groups has been undertaken, a review of the documents submitted by project leaders provides an encouraging preliminary picture. These documents report that teachers experience a heightened sense of professionalism and an improvement in self-esteem as a result of participation in professionally oriented groups of college and school faculty. A number of testimonials indicate, for example, that bright teachers who would have left academic life have decided to remain because of the encouragement they felt as members of academic collaboratives. A number of groups also reported that teachers both at the college and school levels have changed textbooks and realigned curricular objectives after having learned of the work of their colleagues. This indicates that teachers are better able to work toward continuity in the curriculum if they are better informed about expectations and achievements at different levels in the curriculum. Additional testimonials indicate that teachers have changed their individual classroom strategies after being exposed to journal readings in the professional press, and have revised assignments after having participated in writing and reading work with their colleagues in alliance groups.

Principals and deans whose faculty are engaged in Academic Alliances report a heightened sense of responsibility and engagement among their faculty members. They also report their own improved understanding of the discipline because of their involvement with starting alliances and finding incentives for faculty participants. A number of alliance groups have addressed school boards and P.T.A. gatherings with the intention of explaining to them the state of the discipline they teach and its place in the American curriculum. It is likely that when college and school teachers speak with one voice, parents and citizens will listen carefully to the message being conveyed.

Formal evaluation of the impact of academic collaboratives will begin in early 1986.

Conclusions

While the impetus for Academic Alliance groups comes ideally from interested faculty in the discipline, experience indicates the importance of administrators encouraging their faculty to consider the advantages of creating a local community of scholars in their disciplines, and creating incentives designed to make this voluntary commitment more attractive to more faculty members. A handbook on such incentives is being prepared by the central academic office and will be available in January 1986.

But whatever the level of administrative support, successful alliances will require faculty members themselves to overcome deeply ingrained prejudices about one another and to develop respect for one another's knowledge and talents as well as a better understanding of the task each of them undertakes. This is not a rapid process. Most Academic Alliance groups required a year or more of monthly meetings to achieve a mutually

78

satisfying working relationship among the nucleus of members. Given this situation, the creation of Academic Alliances demands patience and sense of mission. For many, this sense of mission grows from the belief that ten years from now Academic Alliances should be a normal part of the life of teachers at all levels. As more faculty commit themselves to intellectual fellowship, American education will be strengthened. Stronger minds will pursue academic careers and more gifted teachers will remain in the classrooms of the nation's schools and colleges.

Claire Gaudiani teaches French and the history and philosophy of science at the University of Pennsylvania. She is assistant director of the Joseph H. Lauder Institute for Management and International Studies at the University of Pennsylvania. She was the director of the project for Strengthening the Humanities through Foreign Language and Literature Studies, and is currently director of the Academic Alliances program. She has authored three books and numerous articles on seventeenth-century French poetry, foreign language pedagogy, humanities education, and management in higher education.

*The Yale-New Haven Teachers Institute demonstrates
that the gap often presumed to exist between university
faculty and school teachers can be bridged by building
an intensive, long-term collaboration to focus on
subjects deemed most important by teachers for
strengthening their own teaching.*

Empowering Teachers as Colleagues: The Yale-New Haven Teachers Institute

James R. Vivian

In the Carnegie Report on high school, E. L. Boyer called for greater emphasis on subject matter in the initial preparation of the teacher and for "a planned continuing education program . . . [as] part of every teacher's professional life" (Boyer, 1983, p. 178). As Boyer later wrote in commenting on the numerous education studies and reports released in 1983, "We are beginning to see that whatever is wrong with America's public schools cannot be fixed without the help of those teachers already in the classrooms. Most of them will be there for years to come, and teachers must be viewed as part of the solution, not as part of the problem" (Boyer, 1984, p. 526).

The State of Teacher Preparation

The needs of teachers in our public schools are compelling. As is the case nationally, a high percentage of teachers in New Haven have minimal formal preparation in their subjects. Only 58.8 percent of New Haven secondary school teachers in the humanities and 36 percent of

W. T. Daly. *College-School Collaboration: Appraising the Major Approaches.* New Directions for
Teaching and Learning, no. 24. San Francisco: Jossey-Bass, December 1985.

secondary school teachers in mathematics and the sciences majored in college or graduate school in the subjects they are teaching. Moreover, because scholarship in these fields is constantly changing, even if a high proportion of teachers had majored in the subjects they teach, they would still need to stay abreast of the developments in their fields.

The present state of teacher preparation in the humanities and the sciences will not be readily improved as a result of new teachers entering the profession. In 1981 nationwide, only 61.9 percent of newly graduated teachers in the arts and humanities and only 43.7 percent of newly graduated teachers in the sciences and mathematics were certified or eligible for certification in the fields they were currently teaching (National Center for Education Statistics, 1983, p. 206). There are already well-publicized shortages of qualified teachers in some subjects and in some areas of the country, even though the National Center for Education Statistics projects that the total demand nationally for secondary school teachers will continue to decline through 1988 (National Center for Education Statistics, 1984). These shortages may well become more widespread and severe at the secondary level as the children of the "baby boomlet," who began this year to increase total elementary school enrollment, begin in the mid-1990s to enter secondary schools (McCarthy, 1984).

In New Haven the current rate of teacher turnover is only about 2 percent. In so stable a teaching force many individuals are reassigned to teach subjects they either have not taught recently, or have never taught before. Furthermore, even in times of higher turnover of teachers, teaching assignments—and therefore teachers' needs for further preparation and new classroom materials—change frequently in response to the shifting priorities of schools, which are so influenced by social and political change.

In short, to strengthen teaching in public schools we must provide for the on-going preparation of individuals already in, and now entering, the profession.

A Microcosm of Urban Education

The demographic characteristics of the New Haven Public Schools mirror urban public education in the United States. In terms of the proportion of the population living below the federally established poverty line, New Haven is the seventh poorest city in the nation. Of the students in New Haven's public secondary schools, more than 60 percent come from families receiving public assistance. The percentage of minority students enrolled in New Haven's public schools is higher than thirty-nine of forty-six major urban school districts surveyed recently. At 83 percent (mostly Black and Hispanic), the rate of minority student enrollment is approximately the same as in Chicago, and higher than in Baltimore, Miami, Philadelphia, Birmingham, Cleveland, and St. Louis (National School Boards Association, 1983). Nationally, the percentage of Black and Hispanic students entering the ninth grade who do not graduate is about twice as great as the proportion of White students who fail to complete high school (National Coalition of Advocates for Students, 1985). In New Haven, 45 percent of individuals entering the ninth grade do not graduate.

As A. Y. Bailey, Vice-President for Academic Affairs of the College Board, points out, "since this demographic pattern [in New Haven] will become increasingly characteristic of public school enrollment throughout the United States, the Yale-New Haven Teachers Institute has chosen, in a sense, to wrestle with the nation's educational future" (Vivian, 1985, p. vii).

A Vested Interest

As Yale President Giamatti has said, "it is profoundly in our self-interest to have coherent, well-taught, well-thought-out curricula" in our local schools and in secondary schools throughout the country. The Institute is important to Yale, in terms of those of its own students coming from New Haven schools, and also in terms of what faculty members who lead Institute seminars gain from the program. They increase their knowledge about public schools and therefore about the educational background of a majority of their own students. Many faculty members also assert that their experience with the Institute has influenced their own teaching and scholarship.

In the absence of a school or department of education, the Institute serves, in effect, as a center for faculty from throughout the institution who care deeply about public education and wish to have a practical, constructive involvement. The Institute draws its faculty from numerous departments of both Yale College and the Graduate School and from the Schools of Architecture, Art, Divinity, Engineering, Forestry and Environmental Studies, Law, and Medicine.

The Institute is also of unquestioned value with respect to the university's relationship with New Haven. In 1984 the University Council on Priorities and Planning wrote: "Yale's principal mission is education. Thus, it seems only natural that Yale concentrate its community efforts upon helping the local public schools meet the enormous challenge of preparing a significantly poor and undereducated population to compete successfully in America's increasingly technical job market" (Council on Priorities and Planning, 1984, pp. 26–27).

The relationship between the university and the schools must be both prominent and permanent within any viable larger relationship between Yale and New Haven; and, of the many ways Yale might aid New Haven, none is more logical than a program that shares Yale's educational resources with the schools. Because of changing student needs, changing objectives set by the school system and each level of government, and changing scholarship, school curricula undergo constant revision. Because of Yale's strength in the academic disciplines, further preparing teachers in the subjects they teach, and assisting teachers to develop curricula and to keep abreast of changes in their fields are the ways that Yale can most readily assist the schools. The intent of the Institute is not, then, to create new resources at Yale; rather, it is to make available in a planned way our existing strength, that is, to expand and to institutionalize the work of university faculty members with their colleagues in the schools.

Governing Principles

The Teachers Institute was established in 1978 as a joint program of Yale University and the New Haven Public Schools, designed to strengthen teaching and thereby to improve student learning in the humanities and the sciences in the community's middle and high schools. Four principles guide the program and constitute much of its distinctiveness. First, teachers of students at different levels can and must interact as colleagues to address the common problems of teaching their disciplines. Second, teacher leadership is crucial in efforts to revitalize public education. Third, teaching is central to the educational process, and teacher-developed materials are essential for student learning, particularly in urban school districts such as New Haven's. Fourth, university-school collaboration must be long-term if it is to be truly effective.

Collegiality. Each year about eighty New Haven school teachers, or almost 25 percent of all secondary teachers in the humanities and the sciences, become Fellows of the Institute to work as colleagues with Yale faculty members on topics the teachers themselves have identified. The Institute is organized to foster collegiality. Through the Institute, teachers become full members of the Yale community and are listed in the university directory of faculty and staff. This has symbolic meaning in recognizing them as colleagues, and practical value in making the human and physical resources of the university accessible to them. Teachers who complete the program successfully receive an honorarium, as well as certification of their course of study, if they are pursuing an advanced degree.

The Institute's demanding five-month program of talks and seminars incorporates the fellows' preparation of new curricular materials that they and other teachers will use in the coming school year. The materials fellows write are compiled into a volume for each seminar and distributed to all New Haven teachers who might use them. Seminar members promote widespread use of these materials by presenting workshops for other teachers during the school year.

A number of the university's most distinguished faculty members have given talks and led seminars in the program. The talks are intended to stimulate thinking and discussion and to point up interdisciplinary relationships in scholarship and teaching. The seminars, which are not regular courses, have the related and equally important purposes of increasing fellows' background and developing new curricular materials on the seminar subjects. As a group, fellows study the seminar subject generally by discussing common readings; individually, each fellow selects a more limited aspect of the subject, and researches and develops it in depth for classroom use. Each seminar must balance these complementary, but in some ways distinct, activities.

Teacher Leadership. In every New Haven middle and high school, teachers serve as representatives of their colleagues in planning and organizing the program. A second group of teachers, Institute Coordinators, coordinates the work of the School Representatives, oversees the conduct of the program, and also has major responsibility for long-range planning, program evaluation, and national dissemination.

Each fall, the school representatives canvass the teachers in their schools to determine the subjects that prospective fellows would like the Institute to treat. The Institute then circulates descriptions of seminars that address teachers' interests, and the institute coordinators, after several meetings with the representatives, ultimately select which seminars will be offered. In effect, New Haven teachers determine the subject matter for the program each year. In applying to the Institute, teachers describe curriculum unit topics on which they propose to work and the relationship of these topics both to Institute seminars and to courses they will teach in the coming school year. In this way, the seminar leaders can tailor the readings and discussions of the seminars to fellows' specific interests and teaching needs.

Long-Term Collaboration. The objective of the Teachers Institute is annually to involve as many school teachers as possible and to offer a range of seminar subjects that span the humanities and the sciences, so that the program can address school curricula, and thus students' education. More than 200 individual teachers have completed the program successfully from one to eight times, and 57 Yale faculty members have given Institute talks or led one or more seminars. Since 1978, the Institute has offered 51 different seminars in the arts and humanities, the social sciences, mathematics, and the physical and life sciences.

In the humanities, Institute offerings have included studies of a particular genre of literature, thematic approaches to literature, seminars on the teaching of writing, and interdisciplinary approaches to literature and history. Additional seminars have examined state and local history, and have focused on recent American, British, or Latin American history. The Institute has also offered several seminars on material culture and architecture. In the social sciences, Institute seminars have explored themes in American adolescence and the American family, often approaching these topics from historical and cross-cultural perspectives. Through various Institute seminars, from architecture to medical imaging, teachers have worked on applications of math, and some seminars have concentrated on math, including statistics. In the sciences, the Institute's work has taken a strongly interdisciplinary approach. Several seminars related study of the physical environment to human biology and human history; others also integrated the physical and life sciences and incorporated advanced medical technology. Through these Institute seminars, fellows have developed more than 430 individual curriculum units for use in school courses.

Curriculum Development. The Institute's approach differs from conventional modes of curriculum development. Classroom teachers, who best know their students needs, work collegially and intensively with Yale faculty members, who are leading scholars in their fields. The Institute does not develop curricula on certain topics only because they are important in terms of recent scholarship; rather, it brings this current knowledge of a field to the assistance of teachers in the areas they identify as their main concerns. The Institute involves no "curriculum experts" in the usual sense, who would themselves prepare new materials, train teachers in short-term workshops to use these materials, and then expect the materials to significantly improve classroom teaching. Instead, the Institute demonstrates that long-term collaboration between school teachers and university scholars can produce teacher generated curriculum materials of high quality pertinent to student needs, and can have a real influence on teaching and learning in the schools.

What fellows write, then, is not "curriculum" in the usual sense. They are not developing content and skill objectives for each course and grade level, nor are they preparing day-by-day lesson plans for their courses. Institute units also differ from traditional curricula in form; they are not composed mainly of lists and outlines of topics to be covered. Rather, teachers research and write in prose on a manageable topic within the seminar subject and describe strategies for introducing that topic in their own teaching.

By writing a curriculum unit, teachers think formally about the ways in which what they are learning can be applied in their own teaching. We emphasize that the Institute experience must have direct bearing on their own classes. This balance between academic preparation and practical, classroom application—as well as the depth and duration of our local collaborative relationship—are central features of the Yale-New Haven Teachers Institute.

Finance

The cost of the Institute stems from our belief that the program is, for university and school participants, a vital professional activity for which they should be remunerated accordingly. Yale and New Haven schools together support a major share of the total cost of the program. A considerable portion of the remaining need has been met through strong support from the National Endowment for the Humanities. We have been pleased also to receive operating funds from numerous foundations and corporations—including more than fifty local businesses which see our efforts to improve the public schools as important to the economic development of our city and region.

In 1982, after five years of developing the Teachers Institute as a model of university-school collaboration, Yale and the schools decided to seek a $4 million endowment to give the program a secure future. The present endowment campaign underscores our deep belief in the long-term significance of the Teachers Institute to the university and to our community's public schools. It also represents our determination to demonstrate that effective collaborative programs can be not only developed, but also sustained.

Evaluation

Our evaluation practices thus far have included four principal activities: (1) review by outside consultants; (2) written evaluation by all participants; (3) surveys of curriculum unit use; (4) and a system-wide analysis of the program using lengthy questionnaires with many responses that are quantifiable. The results of these evaluations offer real encouragement that collaborative programs can assist our schools in specific ways.

Consultants. The annual evaluations by outside consultants have been particularly gratifying. In his report in 1981, E. L. Boyer wrote: "The impact of the Yale-New Haven Teachers Institute far exceeded my expectations. . . Rarely does [school-college collaboration] get to the heart of the matter—helping teachers and advancing the quality of education. The Yale-New Haven teacher project is a dramatic exception to this rule."

T. R. Sizer wrote in his report in 1983:

> I share the view of my predecessor "visitors" that yours is a remarkable program, for its clear and useful focus, for its simplicity and—above all else—for the atmosphere of constructive collegiality between Yale and New Haven teachers that has been created . . . The arguments for the current scale are powerful. All too few school "reform" efforts get the scale right; almost universally they are too ambitious.

N. C. Francis evaluated the program in 1984. He wrote in his report:

> [The] experience and current presence [of the Teachers Institute] as a cooperative venture in and of itself argues for the absolute need for it to continue to be an example of how these difficult change ventures between colleges and universities and schools can be developed and nurtured. Its efforts have inestimable value for a number of local school districts, colleges and universities, all of which are talking about the need to work together, but are uncertain about how and where to start.

District-Wide Study. A comprehensive analysis of the program in 1982 showed that the Institute has significantly increased teachers' knowledge of their disciplines, raised their morale, heightened their expectations of their students' ability to learn, and has in turn improved student learning. About half of the participating teachers reported that the Institute contributed to their decision to continue teaching in our public schools. With respect to the future, only 11 percent of fellows said they did not intend to participate again in the Institute. Eighty percent of teachers who had not been fellows said they would take part, or would consider participating, in the future. This confirms our belief that the Institute will continue annually to attract first-time participants together with former fellows on a recurring basis.

Plans. Over the next three years, the Institute will conduct a series of studies on the ways in which university-school collaboration can strengthen teaching and learning in public schools. Specifically, with the advice and assistance of our national Advisory Committee composed of distinguished educators and philanthropists, we will further investigate the bearing of the Teachers Institute on the preparation, effectiveness, morale, and retention of public school teachers.

Recommendations

The Department of Education recently surveyed over 9,300 school districts nationwide for existing partnerships. Of the 46,000 partnerships they identified, only 5.2 percent are partnerships involving colleges and universities (United States Department of Education, 1985). First, then, we must work not only to sustain the national movement for partnerships in education, but also to increase the participation of colleges and universities within the movement.

There is, in my view, no more important recommendation in the Carnegie Foundation Special Report on school and college (Maeroff, 1983) than the one that calls for universities and schools to develop genuine partnerships based on the needs of schools as determined by their principals and teachers. Both aspects of this recommendation are essential: not only that universities and schools work together, but especially that those of us in higher education encourage our colleagues in schools to show us the ways we can marshal our resources to address their needs.

From our experience in New Haven, I would offer the following guidelines for the successful implementation of the Carnegie recommendation.

Definitions. "Collaboration" is a term currently used to describe quite varied activities. I mean by the term something specific. Collaboration arises from a recognition of mutual interest between school and college—between city and college—that must become more widespread if we are to improve our public schools. Within a partnership of institutions there should be a coequal relationship of colleagues, a volunteer association of individuals who choose to work together, of allies in league to improve our schools. An equal importance must be attached to what each partner brings to the relationship. The aim is to work together without everybody changing place.

Resources. Because institutional and other resources are never adequate, an early step in establishing a collaborative program is to assess the resources that can be made available to meet the needs of schools, and then to apply these resources in an intensive way where the need is greatest. Institutional support must come from both sides of the partnership; tangible and highly visible evidence of such commitment is essential. Participants should be compensated as generously as possible, in order to make their collaboration both demanding and professionally important.

Aims. We especially need to encourage partnerships between schools and colleges and universities that concentrate on teaching and on the continuing engagement of teachers with their fields. Cooperative efforts should insist on a direct application in school classrooms, and not merely assume that their work together will somehow improve teaching and learning in the classroom.

Limitations. A tendency in establishing collaborative programs—as in school reform efforts generally—is to be too ambitious. Programs will succeed only if they have well-defined and manageable goals; they should avoid making impossible claims.

88

Evaluation. Precisely because collaborative projects can achieve only limited, though important, results, participants must be confident that their efforts are worthwhile. An on-going evaluation process is therefore integral to a program's design and should be used perennially to refine both goals and activities. Because collaborative programs are often, unfortunately, seen as nontraditional—because they may not be regarded as central to the mission of either institutional partner—they have a special need to provide sound evidence of their results.

Teacher Leadership. The most successful projects may well begin small, investing real authority in teacher leadership and developing organically based on the needs teachers identify. In that way, programs are not guided by preconceptions, but grow from their own local experience. Efforts at school improvement will not succeed without teacher leadership. In this country we have too long held teachers responsible for the condition of our schools without giving them responsibility—empowering them—to improve our schools.

Duration. For these reasons, and for the benefits to be lasting, effective collaborative programs must be long-term.

Finally, an observation: In universities we assume that on-going scholarship is indispensable to good teaching. The Teachers Institute demonstrates the similar value to school teachers of on-going study and writing about their discipline. Through a collegial relationship with teachers from the university, this continuing engagement with their subjects becomes part of school teachers' professional lives.

References

Boyer, E. L. *High School: A Report on Secondary Education in America.* New York: Harper & Row, 1983.

Boyer, E. L. "Reflections on the Great Debate of '83." *Phi Delta Kappan,* 1984, *66* (8), 525–530.

Council on Priorities and Planning. *Report of the Council on Priorities and Planning, 1983-1984.* New Haven, Conn.: Yale University, 1984.

McCarthy, K. F. *Q's and A's About the Future of the Three R's: A Demographer's Perspective.* Santa Monica, Calif.: The Rand Corporation, 1984.

Maeroff, G. I. *School and College: Partnerships in Education.* Princeton, N.J.: The Carnegie Foundation for the Advancement of Teaching, 1983.

National Center for Education Statistics. *The Condition of Education, 1983 Edition.* Washington, D.C.: National Center for Education Statistics, 1983.

National Center for Education Statistics. *The Condition of Education, 1984 Edition.* Washington, D.C.: National Center for Education Statistics, 1984.

National Coalition of Advocates for Students. *Barriers to Excellence: Our Children at Risk.* Boston: National Coalition of Advocates for Students, 1985.

National School Boards Association. *A Survey of Public Education in the Nation's Urban School Districts.* Washington, D.C.: National School Boards Association, 1983.

United States Department of Education. *Partnerships in Education: Education Trends of the Future.* Washington, D.C.: United States Department of Education, 1985.

Vivian, J. R., and others. *Teaching in America: The Common Ground, A Report of the Yale-New Haven Teachers Institute.* New York: The College Entrance Examination Board, 1985.

James R. Vivian has developed and directed the Yale-New Haven Teachers Institute since its inception in 1977. In 1983 he organized the Yale Conference on the role of colleges and universities in strengthening teaching in public schools, which was attended by chief state school officers and college and university presidents and chancellors from thirty-eight states.

*The Stockton Connection demonstrates the possibility
of translating the latest research developments in all
of the major curricular areas into classroom-useable
materials,* and *the possibility of teaching those content
materials in ways that require students to develop
higher-order thinking skills.*

Continuous Content Updating: The Stockton Connection

William T. Daly
Lucinda Jassel

The Stockton Connection is not a typical collaborative because Stockton
State College is not a typical college. The Connection very much reflects
the college out of which it grew.

The College and the Collaborative

Stockton was established during a very eventful time in higher
education—the end of the 1960s and the beginning of the 1970s—a fact
which shaped decisively its faculty, its curriculum, and its efforts at collaboration with area schools.

The Faculty. Stockton first hired its faculty at a time when there
was a doctoral degree glut on the academic market. In the first year of the
college, there were over 5,000 applications for the initial 55 faculty posi-
tions. The results of this market situation were: a very young faculty,
which looked to local residents like an unruly crowd on the way to a rock

W. T. Daly. *College–School Collaboration: Appraising the Major Approaches.* New Directions for
Teaching and Learning, no. 24. San Francisco: Jossey-Bass, December 1985.

concert; a very powerfully credentialed faculty, with a high percentage of doctoral degrees from the best graduate schools in the country; and a faculty with a pronounced 1960s appetite for uplifting the downtrodden and, in particular, for modifying the traditional disciplinary education they themselves had received in ways that would make it work for a state college student body. Stockton was to make the kind of first-rate liberal arts education, which had been traditionally reserved for well-prepared and well-heeled students, available to state college students at state college prices.

The Curriculum. In pursuit of this goal, the college developed two distinctive curricular structures which were to lead it toward collaboration with area schools. First, we approached liberal arts education not with the traditional distribution requirement among introductory disciplinary courses, but by developing a special set of "General Studies" courses, *each* of which was to be explicitly interdisciplinary. This, as a means of helping state college students to make the connections among major bodies of knowledge that better-prepared students might have been left to make on their own. We also required *all* faculty to contribute one-third of their courses to that special curriculum, and recruited and retained faculty according to their ability to integrate their specialized disciplinary knowledge with knowledge from other areas, and according to their ability to make those interdisciplinary materials interesting and intelligible to students in general and to non-majors in particular. As a result, we developed a sizable number of faculty in virtually every curricular field who were specialists in helping nonspecialists to integrate and make sense of the explosion of specialized knowledge. Second, because of the nature of our student body and the philosophical commitments of our faculty, we were able to build a skills program that eventually involved course contributions from fully one-half of our 170 faculty members. That program was also centered, from its inception, on developing the higher-order *thinking* skills that are increasingly understood to be the underpinning of reading, writing, and mathematical skills. Finally, because both our general education and our skills efforts were based on retraining and redirecting the efforts of our regular faculty, rather than hiring special faculty, we accumulated substantial experience in the in-service training of faculty—or, perhaps more precisely, in helping faculty to continuously and collectively retrain themselves.

The Collaborative. The Stockton Connection began as a suspicion, in the minds of a small group of faculty, that the instructional approaches and materials just described might be precisely what students should be getting *before* they come to college; and that Stockton, largely by accident, might be uniquely equipped to offer to pre-college audiences what it had learned in these areas. We began by trying that notion out on a number of local superintendents. Only one, a new, change-oriented superintendent in a district with many of the problems typical of urban districts, was willing to take the initial gamble. She allowed us to work with a group of her teachers who were developing a new ninth-grade Civics course.

Based on some modicum of success in that project, we persuaded her, and another superintendent in a neighboring urban district, to turn over all seven half-days set aside in their districts for in-service training to a team of Stockton faculty, for the purpose of presenting the instructional techniques and materials that we had developed over a decade of work on our own reasonably successful general education and basic skills programs.

Lumps, Lessons, and Advice

Over the next year of in-service training efforts, this band of bright-eyed educational reformers took a severe drubbing. The lessons from this drastically altered our approach to collaborative work, and are offered here to other pilgrims who are interested in collaborative projects. Those lessons were taught, appropriately, by the teachers with whom we worked.

Self-Selection. They explained to us, sometimes gently and sometimes not, that most teachers viewed the traditional in-service training days as in-school detention for teachers—in no small part because attendance was required of everyone whether or not they were interested in the topic under discussion. Lesson number one: Structure collaborative activities so that only those teachers who want to be there are there.

Content over Method. The teachers also made it clear that they had had more than enough work on teaching methods in their undergraduate and graduate education courses, most of which they viewed as being a good deal less useful than practical classroom experience. They thought we *might,* however, be able to provide them with some help in keeping up with developments in their content areas—particularly because many of them had been assigned to teach in areas in which they had little formal preparation, and because their heavy teaching load (unlike our luxurious one) left them with little time for keeping up. Lesson number two: Build your collaborative effort so that college faculty can make a contribution in the area of their greatest strength, their grasp of the latest content area developments, and teachers can make their contribution in the area of their greatest strength, their understanding of the best ways to make instruction work in the classroom.

Incrementalism. The teachers explained to us that several half-days of in-service training, scattered over the academic year, were insufficient to have any real impact on classroom instruction. Teachers, for the most part, suffer those sessions with outside "experts" the way peasants suffer bad weather; they "hunker" down and wait for it to end. Lesson number three: If a collaborative effort is to have any real impact on instruction, it must be intensive enough to fully engage teachers as intellectuals, and extended enough so that piecemeal change in instructional materials and approaches can accumulate over time to become significant change.

Don't Ask, Do It. In response to our repeated and appropriately humble questions about what they most needed, the teachers suggested, with some impatience, such things as better-prepared and better-disciplined students, smaller classes, higher pay, and the intimidation or selective assassination of some members of the administration. Above all, they most needed to be left alone by do-gooders with stupid questions. Lesson number four: Teachers, like most garden-variety human beings, spend most of their time worrying about their most pressing problems— about most of which the best-intentioned college faculty can do little. They are not going to provide much spontaneous guidance in response to purely academic questions. If you have an academic service that you think might be useful to them, define it, try to get a few hearty souls to try some of it, and *then* listen very carefully to their response.

Description

At the end of this year of in-service work we scrapped that approach to collaboration and began afresh. The current version of the Stockton Connection directly reflects what the teachers taught us. It is built around several guiding principles.

Self-Selection. Quality education depends, ultimately, on the relationships between teachers and their students. Centrally mandated testing programs can measure education success but they cannot produce it. Administration-mandated in-service programs, even with the best curricular materials, will have little effect if they are not understood and embraced by the classroom teacher. As a result, the teacher remains the central determinant of effectiveness in education. And with teachers, only external compliance can be mandated. Excellence must be supported and nurtured—over a long period of time.

In light of this understanding, we moved our collaborative efforts out of the framework of mandated in-service training into voluntary summer seminars, and began to work only with those teachers who were interested in working with us.

Content over Method. The most pressing need of most classroom teachers is for on-going content-area updates, organized in such a way as to require students to think. The knowledge explosion now occurring in many academic fields only very slowly and imperfectly makes an impact on textbook construction and adoption. In addition, the teaching load and reward system for elementary and secondary school teachers provides little of the support available to college faculty for keeping up with the latest developments in their fields. The resulting gap between what is happening at the cutting edges of the various disciplines and what is available to classroom teachers, if it continues to grow unchecked, will steadily impoverish the quality of the education that students receive. Many teachers will also be understandably reluctant to go beyond memorization of text materials and formulas into the less-controlled techniques necessary to teach students to think independently and critically—until their own standing as up-to-date authorities on the subject matter is secure and clearly visible to the students.

As a result of this understanding, the Stockton Connection focuses on bringing to middle and high school faculty continuing updates on the most recent developments in the various content areas—selected, summarized, and simplified with an eye to classroom use, and organized and presented in such a way as to require students to develop higher-order thinking skills in order to come to grips with the material. This latter emphasis on thinking skills reflects two beliefs: (1) There is growing evidence that a single set of thinking skills may underlie effective reading, writing, and even quantitative abilities, and that the lack of those thinking skills may be at the root of the broader problem of skills deficiencies among many high school graduates. (2) The same knowledge explosion that has created the need among teachers for continuous content updates has also created the need among their students, as citizens in the making, for the general analytical skills necessary to manage and make use of that knowledge explosion.

Incrementalism. The fate of many of the new curricula developed in the post-Sputnik era indicates that sweeping curricular change is likely to be resisted. It is difficult to digest and assimilate, and teachers might be right in believing that materials and techniques which they have developed by trial and error to suit their particular clientele ought not to be readily cast aside in favor of unproven alternatives. As already indicated, however, we have come to share some of the widespread skepticism among teachers about the effectiveness of the much more limited practice of scattering a handful of all-school, in-service days across the school year.

The Stockton Connection, as a result, falls somewhere between the current approach to in-service and earlier attempts at sweeping curricular reform. Our summer seminars focus on the development of specific blocks of material which either can be used as supplemental material or can be integrated, piecemeal, into the existing curriculum. With respect to those blocks of material, however, we do require intensive and extended work. Specifically, the summer seminars begin with an intensive week of instruction in which Stockton faculty members summarize the latest and most important developments in each of a number of major curricular areas, and suggest ways in which those materials might be presented in order to emphasize the development of student thinking skills. That is followed by a month of independent study in which the teachers translate those new content materials into instructional modules for classroom use. The final component of the seminar is another intensive week at the college during which these attempts to marry recent and sophisticated content materials with effective classroom instruction are collectively reviewed and revised. During the following fall and early winter, Stockton faculty meet with seminar participants to discuss their classroom experience with these new materials—what worked, and what did not. As a result of this set of meetings, a summary of the content material presented by the Stockton faculty member, together with the most effective lessons participating teachers developed for carrying those materials into the classroom, is written up in booklet form. This information is then disseminated to wider audiences by two methods: (1) spring in-service sessions in the participating districts, presented jointly by Stockton faculty and participating teachers; and (2) a statewide conference hosted each March by Stockton.

Evaluation

The Stockton Connection has completed two years of experience in its second incarnation. It is still a bit early for celebration. But the initial auguries are positive.

Enrollments. The first set of summer seminars attracted 45 teachers from 15 districts. The districts were clearly doing the sensible thing; they sent us a few scouts. The March conference which grew out of that first batch of small seminars, however, drew over 300 participants from 96 districts statewide. Participation in a conference is, of course, a minimal commitment, and the skeptics suggested that the free lunch might be sufficient to account for the large number of attendees. But enrollment for the second set of summer seminars tripled to include 150 participants, with enrollment in many of the seminars closing very early. We had clearly struck a responsive chord.

Participant Evaluation. The second set of summer seminars was evaluated by means of an anonymous questionnaire, ostentatiously sealed to indicate they would be read only after grades had been submitted. On a 7-point scale, the mean score for the effectiveness of the Stockton instructors was 6.3. The comparable number for the effectiveness of the seminar was 6.0. The dominant response on the open-ended questions was that the seminars were very good but also *very* demanding of time and effort.

It is not yet clear whether that last dual evaluation will fill seats or empty them. Neither is it clear how much long-term change for the better in actual classroom instruction will be achieved. The Stockton Connection is a high-risk, high-gain venture. The seminar offerings are dictated more by the direction of developments in the major areas of knowledge than by expressed teacher demand. The seminars are also intensive and impose a substantial time and effort burden on teachers, many of whom must work at least part time in the summer in order to sustain themselves. Finally, because Stockton is an entirely undergraduate college, teachers must assume those burdens without the benefit of graduate credit. As a result, the Connection is less well adapted to reflecting current instructional practices and teacher preferences than it is to transforming them.

The Stockton Connection is now four years old, and is, because of its nature, unlikely to have a long and uneventful existence. Before the next four years have passed, it is likely to either soar or crash.

William T. Daly is a professor of political science at Stockton State College, chairman of the New Jersey Task Force on Thinking Skills, and the founder and director of the Stockton Connection Collaborative.

Lucinda Jassel is an instructor in political science at Stockton State College, director of Stockton's Freshman Year Program, and a founding member of the Stockton Connection Collaborative.

PART 4.

Getting Started

The Metropolitan Area Schools Project offers a model,
for those interested in initiating collaboratives, of
building collaboration up from the expressed needs
of the constituencies it is designed to serve.

Multiple Services on Request: The University of Missouri-Kansas City's Metropolitan Area Schools Project

Deanna C. Martin

Two words are prominent among current educational buzzwords: "collaboration" and "partnerships." Everybody who is anybody is in the act, either as a collaborator or as a partner in some kind of endeavor to improve American education. Lest the reader suspect a hint of hyperbole here, please note the following.

At the June 1985 White House Conference on Partnerships in Education (PIE), Fred Ryan, Director of PIE and Deputy Assistant to the President, reported that since President Reagan proclaimed 1983–1984 as the National Year of Partnerships in Education, over 46,000 partnerships had been documented. According to Ryan, the presidential proclamation had struck a resonant chord; business, agencies, and organizations, as well

W. T. Daly. *College-School Collaboration: Appraising the Major Approaches.* New Directions for
Teaching and Learning, no. 24. San Francisco: Jossey-Bass, December 1985.

as individuals, had risen to meet the challenge. Forty-six thousand in twenty months since the President signed the document—an average of 920 per state.

An exaggeration? Well, of course, but those of us in the audience were willing to let it stand. Credit for this "new initiative" aside, the important point was that President had *named* it, and by naming it had given an otherwise amorphous, divergent, unfocused effort an identity and a charge. In a sense, the milling crowd had become a marching army.

A Context for Change

Any educational movement that erupts with enough vitality to command both local and national support has likely been fermenting for some time.

The Community. Certainly collaborations existed in Kansas City as they have elsewhere for decades. Foundations and civic councils in our city care both philosophically and pragmatically about the quality of local education. Those who seek to attract new business and industry to the area are particularly concerned. Potential investors are interested in the quality of public education in Kansas City. Those families they recruit from other cities demand access to good schools; the quality of local education bears heavily upon the quality of the local labor pool. For example, the fact that the Kansas City Public School District (KCPSD) continues to be in the throes of a desegregation suit discourages economic development. Civic leaders, therefore, are eager to support educational reform. The question is, what to support? And to what extent? Or, as one crusty philanthropist put it, "Where can we get the most bang for our bucks?"

The University. The establishment of some sort of organized institutional effort was also in the interest of the University of Missouri-Kansas City (UMKC). Both individuals and institutions compete for the local precollege program dollars aimed at strengthening public education. In grant and contract competition, the university has been represented largely by faculty from the School of Education. Faculty of other university schools and departments have participated in pre-collage education through service activities, as either paid consultants or volunteers. Overall, such involvement has been sporadic with each faculty member taking a proprietary view of his or her own particular effort. Certainly there has been no central coordinating agent within the university; no one responsible for articulating a common goal, nor anyone responsible for evaluation or quality control. Moreover, credit for such activities has accrued to the individuals involved—rarely to the university.

The Federal Government. Finally, federal policy has also served to direct interest toward local collaboration and partnerships. President Reagan sought to decentralize education and cut federal funding. The status reports on the quality of American education confirmed everyone's worst fears. Federal money was offered as an incentive to improve the quality of math and science education in an effort to assure a competitive American market. Stipulations promoting local partnerships were built into the funding guidelines of the major federal agencies. Private foundations such as the Ford Foundation also encouraged collaboration by offering "seed money" for partnerships between urban universities and urban public schools.

Local partners were available, federal and foundation incentives were present, and a high level of interest existed in all quarters of the community. It is within this context, with these prevailing attitudes that the UMKC Metropolitan Area Schools Project (MASP) began.

Organizational Strategy

The uniqueness of MASP is in its organization. A description of that aspect is possibly of greater potential benefit to the reader than the program components themselves. As educators we learned long ago that it is folly to take a program developed within a single context and try to transport it intact to another site. Such an attempt is analogous to capturing a beautiful mosaic within a kaleidoscope and trying to carry it across the room for someone else to see. Once you get it there, it still may be beautiful but it will not be the same mosaic. The reader, therefore, will find more information about the way we planned the collaborative than about specific program areas. What follows is a narrative history of the project's development.

The Assignment. When the directive came from UMKC's Chancellor, it was loosely defined: The partnership project was to focus on the improvement of inner-city math and science education and was to be campus-wide in scope. Only weeks before, however, the chancellor had approved a year-long leave for the Dean of the School of Education to serve as special consultant to the Superintendent of the Kansas City Public School District. This action, more than any other, confirmed his seriousness of purpose—to the UMKC faculty and to the community at large.

Metropolitan Scope. Although both the chancellor and the Ford Foundation had charged the urban university to support the urban schools, the MASP staff determined at this point that we could be of most help to the Kansas City Public School District if we approached the effort as a metropolitan, area-wide project. We thought that as long as the Kansas City Public School District remained cut off from suburban districts and their resources, talents, and optimism, our job would be impossible. What the urban district needed was substantive, broad-based support that was sufficient to capture attention and raise expectations. The project had to be bold. It had to be imaginative. It had to promise long-lasting commitments instead of quick fixes.

The Role of Broker. Most important, the project had to respond to district needs *as those needs were perceived by district teachers and administrators.* Essentially, we saw ourselves in the role of broker. We decided to commit our campus resources to projects that had the widest possible base of support, in the belief that the greater the number of constituencies owning an idea, the better its chance for success. That meant to us, for example, that both the superintendent and the teachers should agree on the nature and scope of a project. Since most of us had been public school teachers, we knew from experience that quality of communication between teachers and their superintendents is often less than ideal. Both groups are quite capable of solving educational problems; however, they rarely talk to one another, and when they do, the proverbial spear is often in the ground. Solutions emanating from either group are likely to be discounted and distrusted by the other. We also knew from experience that both groups are likely to view with suspicion solutions offered by "outside experts." We certainly did not want to assume that role. Perhaps, we reasoned, we could generate dialogue, collect ideas, and sift through them to identify possible areas of agreement or "matches." Then, perhaps, we could act as a broker for them.

As we worked to broker matches *among* districts, we consciously expanded the concept of "collaborative" beyond the triad of inner-city schools, urban university, and private sector, adding the suburban districts as a fourth partner in the program. Surely we could identify some educational concerns common to several of our thirteen public school districts. This, too, had to be carefully considered because of the desegregation suit and the surrounding legal implications. Additionally, we wanted to include two large districts that were very near the university but were actually across the state line in Kansas. Inclusion of these would cause some jurisdictional problems; however, if we were successful in agreeing on some common causes, our chances to gain local, state, and federal support would be much enhanced. What none of us could do alone might be accomplishedd if we approached the problems together as an organized collaborative.

The Vice-Chancellor Goes Calling. We wanted the collaborative to be perceived as a legitimate, university program rather than as a service effort on the part of a few individual faculty members. Consistent with that view, we initiated MASP through a series of outreach visits. Instead of inviting the public school superintendents to come to our campus to discuss potential collaboration, we decided we could set the appropriate tone and get a better sense of the issues that might be addressed through the collaborative if the university's chief academic officer called on each superintendent. Appointments were set. The opening message was always the same: "What can the university do for you?"

The discussions generated three observations: (1) common educational concerns among the districts did exist; (2) rarely did the superintendents discuss their problems or proposed solutions with one another; (3) both our project and the idea of collaboration seemed welcome. Several superintendents, however, were quite direct in asking what the university stood to gain from this initiative. The answer was equally direct: better-educated entry-level university students, teacher training opportunities, a better reputation for the university in the community, a better-informed university faculty, and shared revenue from grants and contracts.

At the conclusion of each meeting, we asked the superintendent if he would be willing to meet with his peers and interested university faculty and staff to discuss issues of common concern. Each agreed. We also asked if he would mind our inviting some key teachers to the university to discuss math and science needs with university representatives and teachers from other districts. None objected, and some offered the names of teachers who should be invited.

During some of these meetings, needs arose that could be met immediately. We did so and, in this way, were able to promptly demonstrate the seriousness of the university's commitment to the improvement of education.

The Roundtable, the Teacher Councils, and Near Disaster. Within three months, we had organized the Superintendents' Roundtable. The $2,500 in seed money had been secured through the National Association of State Universities and Land-Grant Colleges (NASULGC), and we were negotiating the final details of a $50,000 grant from a local foundation. The latter funds were to be used to purchase released time for faculty, technical assistance for writing further grant applications, travel, and a part-time project assistant to oversee the day-to-day operation of the collaborative. All the essentials appeared to be in place for the official launching.

The outcome of the first meeting of the Superintendents' Roundtable threatened to end the project. In planning the meeting, we had been extremely conservative. The agenda included *safe* topics of mutual interest such as curriculum revision, in-service needs, and new state requirements for graduation. Nothing radical. Nothing we could not handle with existing resources. What we did *not* count on was activism among this group.

After the agenda had been dealt with, one superintendent proposed what was to become the Mathematics and Physics Institute—a program to bring gifted students together in a cooperative, interdistrict program for work that went beyond the usual high school curricular offerings. Three other superintendents agreed to support the idea.

Two weeks later, when the first meeting of teacher representatives from the districts was scheduled, fifty math teachers attended. We asked them to divide into small groups to discuss their hopes, dreams, frustrations, and to compile a list of specific ideas they believed would improve the quality of math education in the Kansas City area. Before they divided into groups, however, somebody asked for an explanation of a rumor he had heard. Was it true that we were about to establish a new program for gifted math and science students that would take the students out of their schools and transport them to the university campus for instruction? In spite of explanations the teachers were furious, asserting that the superintendents had, in the interest of collaboration, sold out to the university.

What we had tried most to avoid had occurred. Although that one program is still dealing with negative repercussions, we were lucky not to have caused a walkout and subsequent boycott by the teachers. It appeared to them that in one move we had taken their best students away, eliminated their prized teaching assignments, jeopardized their status as teachers of the gifted, and according to one, robbed him of the one and only bright spot in his day. All this without so much as consulting a single teacher.

At the time, we handled the crisis the only way we knew how: we listened and we sympathized. We also tried to assure them that the superintendents and the university had every intention of including them in the new endeavor. While this was true, our after the fact explanation was not very satisfying to us or anyone else. That blunder aside, the math teachers, and later another fifty equally offended science teachers, granted us the cooperation we sought.

In each meeting, we listed and ranked the priority of the educational concerns. At the conclusion of the evening's efforts, we asked the teachers if they would be willing to work on one of the identified problems. We knew that the meetings had been initially successful when we saw how difficult it was for our colleagues to narrow their decision down to one choice. These teacher commitments, then, became the basis for the Teacher Councils. In all, three math and three science councils developed, each one focusing on a problem that the teachers had identified and that had also been identified independently through the Superintendents' Roundtable. Not surprisingly, there was great similarity in the problems identified by both groups.

Program Components

With regard to the Teacher Councils, the major concerns have been curriculum reform and in-service training. For example, one math council is in the process of completing a grant proposal that would establish an area-wide kindergarten through twelfth grade coordinated math curriculum. This proposal will soon be ready to go into negotiations with each of the seven superintendents who originally indicated interest in the project. Similarly, another council has established the Kansas City Science Curriculum Project, which involves five districts. The curriculum development process that they will pursue will be quite different. Two other councils are developing plans to address teacher in-service needs; the councils have conducted area-wide surveys and are now negotiating for additional university courses and for specific in-service programs. Finally, area teachers have jointly developed a concept paper for a Science and Math Resources Center Council. At present there is no resource center in the Kansas City area for teachers and students to gain access to science and math materials.

In addition to the councils and the Roundtable, the following have been realized as a direct result of the collaborative.

Career Exploration Project. Jointly sponsored by UMKC, the Kansas City Public School District, and the Coalition of 100 Black Women, this project seeks to provide summer work and educational programs for 100 disadvantaged high school juniors from the nine KCPSD high schools. Area employers serve as personal mentors to those students whom they employ.

Elementary Science Coordinators. A faculty member of the UMKC Biology Department served a three-semester term as an elementary science coordinator to one of the local suburban districts. The district is now satisfied that one of its own teachers can assume this new role, and is in the process of negotiating a joint appointment in another area of need. Requests for joint appointments from other districts are being considered, as are plans to reverse the process by bringing district teachers and administrators to the university for extended fellowships.

A final word about the Mathematics and Physics Institute. In spite of its rocky beginning, this program has turned out to be a great success. Last fall, sixty-nine gifted students from nine high schools enrolled in college-level physics and calculus taught jointly by university and high school faculty. Because of its innovative nature and the degree of satisfaction expressed by those involved, other districts are already requesting membership in the institute. We will entertain the idea of expansion after another year of operation.

Evaluation and Advice

Because our organizational strategy put us in a service mode from the outset, there have not been the traditional false starts and blind alleys that have besieged other beginning efforts. The tasks that we have undertaken have had the support to move forward. As a center, we are in the habit of making both formative and summative evaluations. Data collected from program participants and recipients have indicated above-average satisfaction.

Personnel. Our greatest concern, one of manpower and financial resources, remains; we are definitely overcommitted. Even though the local foundation funded our proposal, and a "deepening" grant through NASULGC allowed us to hire a full-time coordinator, MASP has put an alarming drain on Center resources. If, however, center staff had not been available, this entire effort would have been in serious trouble within the first six weeks. By then, we had talked to superintendents representing a total of 306 public schools and 149,482 students. As mentioned above, we wanted to honor every request that was feasible, and by the time we had completed our visits, the commitments far exceeded the availability of faculty and staff time assigned to MASP.

Regarding manpower, there was another lesson to learn. While it was easy to take comfort from the thought that the university has over 700 faculty, the truth is that when one needs a quality job done, one tends to lean on people with a track record of top performance. These few on any campus are well known to all, and competition for their time is fierce. We did get support from most of those we asked, but in general universities are not structured to reward such efforts; therefore, experienced faculty must consider service requests in relation to their other professional priorities. Similarly, talented junior faculty cannot afford the luxury of accepting service assignments because of the publish-or-perish requirements for promotion and tenure. The whole situation, as far as faculty support is concerned, is difficult to negotiate.

On the positive side, we have continued to receive financial support and positive press and encouragement from the community. The chancellor has formalized MASP by according it status as one of his top five priorities and by allocating dollars to the effort.

Collective Wisdom and Consensus. Overall, we believe that MASP finds strength in its organizational framework. Chief administrators from both the university and the public school districts are involved, as are university faculty and public school teachers. Moreover, two other local educational resource agencies have joined the consortium.

Decisions are based on collective wisdom and consensus. In this way, participants can feel some assurance that their energies will not be wasted. Perhaps the greatest obstacle to overcome is the question of credibility, especially among teachers and faculty who have for years seen efforts at educational reform go nowhere.

Communication. Among the most serious problems are those involving communication. Sometimes it seems that everyone wants to be kept up to date on everything. At other times, no one has time to read mail or attend a meeting. The MASP staff are responsible for ensuring that those who need to know do know, and those who need to be asked are asked, and those who need to sign off, sign off. We have not found written communication to be an effective medium, however, except as a record of verbal agreements. We try to negotiate all sensitive issues in person, and to conduct everyday business by phone. We have also learned to do what physicians' offices do: Call everyone the day before a meeting as a reminder. This makes a substantial difference in attendance, especially among teachers.

Networking. Finally, not only does the MASP Director need reliable assistance at the local level, he or she also needs advice from colleagues in the field. Publications such as this collection are only now beginning to emerge. Support networks that we have found particularly helpful include NASULGC (One Dupont Circle, Washington, D.C. 20036) and the National Symposium on Partnerships in Education (Office of Private Sector Initiatives, The White House, 1600 Pennsylvania Avenue NW, Washington, D.C. 20500).

When "Nation at Risk" came out, most of us expected that the President would be forced to back down from his opposition to federal fiscal support for education. He did not. Instead, he called for private sector initiatives; anyone who is still sitting back waiting for federal funding to save the day will have a long, long wait. Collaboration may not be the game one would prefer, but for the present, it is the only game in town; and for the foreseeable future, it offers the best hope for meaningful change.

Deanna C. Martin directs the Center for Academic Development of the University of Missouri-Kansas City. When the University undertook to establish a collaborative program with the public schools and the private sector, she was selected to develop that project which became the Metropolitan Area Schools Project.

PART 5.

Projections

The "crisis" in American education is a major opportunity for the most venturesome of American educators. Education in general and collaborative education in particular will find increasing levels of political and financial support.

The Time Is Now: Educating Citizens for a High-Tech World

William T. Daly

As a user's manual, this volume has focused on various *ways* of going about collaborative education. Perhaps an even greater question than the effectiveness of particular methods of collaboration, in the minds of many educators, is the question of whether *any* new ventures of this type should be undertaken in the midst of very uncertain times for educational institutions. School-age and college-age populations are declining, federal funding is drying up, and a veritable snowstorm of national reports has deplored the quality of both pre-collegiate and collegiate education. Educators might reasonably conclude that this is a particularly good time to hunker down, avoid new ventures, or perhaps get out of the education profession entirely.

The purpose of this concluding chapter is to argue that the current crisis in American education is, on the contrary, a major opportunity for the most venturesome among American educators. The very amount of attention now being paid to the country's education system, and the fact that the authors of the national reports include business and political leaders as well as educators, reflect the rediscovery in times of economic

W. T. Daly. *College-School Collaboration: Appraising the Major Approaches.* New Directions for Teaching and Learning, no. 24. San Francisco: Jossey-Bass, December 1985.

adversity of what had been forgotten during the post-war economic boom. An effective educational system is essential to three things that Americans have always valued more than they have valued enlightenment for its own sake: the opportunity for individual advancement, an internationally competitive and prosperous economy, and political and social stability.

It is this understanding by those with power and money that has produced the current criticism of the educational system. It is this understanding that will produce growing political and financial support for reform initiatives.

The Roots of the Crisis

Opportunity has been at the root of the three major promises that America has traditionally made to its citizens. Education has been the central mechanism for making good on those promises.

America has promised *individual opportunity* for self-improvement and advancement. It has promised economic *prosperity* based on a free market economy, which is powered by that desire for individual advancement, and which continuously allocates and reallocates the resultant human effort to its most efficient uses. And, in return for their consent to be governed, it has promised citizens *democratic participation* in making the decisions they are expected to obey.

The American educational system was to offer all the opportunity for self-transformation and improvement, to provide the trained workforce necessary for economic prosperity, and to provide the shared values and knowledge necessary to an informed and responsible citizenry.

The sheer size of the post-war economic boom itself made good on most of those promises, and thus saved those of us in education from any serious test of how well we were perfrming our societal functions. The booming economy seemed capable of assuring a substantial amount of individual opportunity and economic prosperity regardless of what our students learned or did not learn. And the seemingly endless expansion of the economy saved the political system from many of the difficult decisions on distribution that might otherwise have tested the effectiveness of our citizenship training.

The emergence of Europe, Japan, and even a number of Third World countries as major economic competitors has slowed the growth of the American economy. The current wave of criticism and debate over American education reflects nothing less fundamental than the end of the post-war boom. This has resulted in scrutiny of the educational system's ability to make good on America's three promises under a more demanding set of economic and political conditions.

Part of what must be done educationally, particularly with respect to restoring the international competitiveness of the American economy, must be done at major research universities—the institutions best-equipped to generate new knowledge and products. But much of what must be done to maintain individual opportunity for advancement, to educate a technically literate workforce, and to sustain an informed citizenry must be undertaken as a joint mission by the schools and undergraduate colleges—the institutions best equipped to broadly disseminate new knowledge.

More specifically, our joint pursuit of all three of those objectives will require the revival of an old idea and the introduction of a new one. The old idea, rendered current once again by the rapid generation and obsolescence of knowledge, is that it is at least as important to teach students how to think, and hence how to learn continuously, as it is to teach them specific content knowledge. The new idea, necessitated by that same avalanche of important but short-lived knowledge, is that the teaching of specific content knowledge must increasingly be carried out as a continuing series of updates.

Those two ideas, as some of the recent national reports on higher education have already suggested, will require a significicnt portion of the nation's college faculty to move back toward teaching as its primary function, and hence toward its colleagues in the elementary and secondary schools. Specifically, many of us at the college level will have to abandon our attempts to imitate the major research universities and instead focus on the equally important task of aggregating the flood of new knowledge they generate, usually in highly specialized dribs and drabs, and presenting it in ways that are intelligible and interesting to the average student and citizen.

While it is the central thrust of this chapter to argue that there will be opportunities and support for those who wish to move in the direction just described, there will also be temptations aplenty to offer more short-sighted responses to the current crisis with respect to all three of the societal functions which American education has traditionally served.

Individual Opportunity

The promise of individual opportunity for self-improvement and advancement has been central to American society ethically, economically, and politically. It has provided the central ethical justification for paying the inevitable human costs associated with an individualistic and competitive society. It has provided the economic system with a generally optimistic and energetic workforce. And it has helped to ensure political stability, even during hard times, by holding out to poor people the hope of improvement for themselves and their children.

In an attempt to make good on our part of that promise, those of us in education have steadily expanded the definition of students' educational rights at the pre-college level and steadily expanded access to higher education—at some price in terms of the quality of education which students receive.

There is now a growing temptation to solve the problem of educational quality the easy way—by restricting access. The mechanisms are already available and a powerful case can be made, in the name of "standards," for using them. Poorly prepared students can be placed onto "tracks" where little is expected of them, or of their teachers, and they can then be excluded from higher education by increasing admissions standards. This, however, is a questionable approach—not only ethically but politically. It must be remembered that the expansion of access to education resulted from social conflict as well as social conscience. And removing opportunity, once it has been offered, is often even more explosive than denying it in the first place. Happily, such a retreat from the principle of equal opportunity is unnecessary.

Two very promising developments are now emerging as a result of two decades of research and experimentation born of the need to work with poorly prepared students. They should be pursued, not abandoned, as a part of the current drive to raise educational standards. First, the current boom in research on reasoning skills reflects emerging, though still scattered, evidence that a single set of reasoning skills may underlie the capacities for efficient, selective reading, for effective writing, *and* even for success in many quantitatively based scientific areas. If that is true, and if we can confirm the early indications that such reasoning skills are teachable, we may be able to fashion a short-cut to academic competence for poorly prepared students and thus maintain high educational standards without closing off access to education. At the same time, the growing capacity of computers to store, retrieve, and organize information, together with great strides in simplifying the use of computers, may permit us to give educationally disadvantaged students a similar short-cut to informational resources that have until now been the exclusive property of their more fortunate peers. Increasingly, we should be able to *both* raise the standards that students must meet once they are in the educational system *and* help the most motivated of disadvantaged students measure up to such rigorous standards.

If this is the case, there should be increasing amounts of support available not only for the collaboratives discussed in previous chapters that are designed for well-prepared students, but also for the others that are designed to help their more poorly prepared peers.

Economic Prosperity

While the global debate over the relative merits of planned and free-market economics continues, the strong suit of free-market economies (in their competitive sectors) is clearly their decentralized decision-making and their resultant ability to effectively make the decisions that collectively allocate and reallocate people and resources to their most efficient use. As the rate of technological change accelerates, one of the major challenges to the educational system will be to train a workforce creative and flexible enough to lead, or at least adapt to, that accelerating rate of change.

If much of the current talk about "technical literacy" and "high-tech education" leads, at both the pre-college and college levels, only to the growth of more and more highly specialized technical education, we will do our students a disservice and contribute to the continuing decline of America's international economic position. If "high tech" means anything, it means *change*. Specialized educational content, particularly in technical fields, will quickly become obsolete. And, once new products are ready for mass production, even in high-tech industries, many of the production jobs will migrate to less developed countries where labor and resources are cheaper—a process already underway.

There is a growing and persuasive body of economic thought which argues that the economic prosperity of the industrialized states, with their high levels of education and high labor costs, will increasingly depend on their capacity to develop and *initially* exploit an endless series of new opportunities and products. The ability to do that will depend on an educational system that *both* produces a professional workforce with the broad areas of competence and general intellectual skills necessary to continuous learning, *and* provides them with the opportunity for continuous technical retraining to meet specific emerging needs.

If this projection is accurate, the emphasis on the broad liberal arts education and on the development of broadly applicable intellectual skills present in both the national reports on education and in many of the collaboratives discussed in the preceding pages, may be not only good education but also good economics.

Citizenship

Democracy has a practical as well as a philosophical justification. People are more likely to obey government decisions if they feel they have some opportunity to participate in shaping the decisions they are expected to obey. Political participation therefore has always been related not only to political justice but also to political stability.

The upheavals of the 1960s were warning tremors—indicating that large numbers of citizens at both the upper and lower ends of the income scale had lost faith in their ability to influence decisions through established channels and in the moral legitimacy of the decisions being made by government. While the cities and the campuses have since fallen silent, public opinion polls continue to indicate declining levels of public belief in both the responsiveness and the fairness of government. Voting levels, perhaps as a result of these perceptions, remain alarmingly low.

This already weakened and creaking structure of citizen support for government is now being placed under additional strain by two new problems. The explosion of new knowledge, and the resultant ascendance of the "experts," threatens to further undermine citizens' confidence in their ability to understand and influence public policy. And the end of the post-war economic boom increasingly forces us to make tough decisions about the distribution of scarce resources. These decisions are perhaps the most difficult test of any people's trust in the fairness of their government. Nor will the current economic recovery absolve us of the need to make such difficult decisions—as the disagreements over different approaches to reducing the federal deficit make clear.

Historically, such a loss of citizen efficacy and of moral legitimacy has often lead to apathy and cynicism about government, in good economic times, and to an appetite for simplistic, intolerant, and even violent solutions to intractable problems, in bad times. There is no reason to believe that America will be immune to such a pattern should we permit similar conditions to arise.

Tempting as it may sometimes seem, we cannot respond by simply reaffirming for the public the traditional virtues of the American system in the traditional way, and leaving it to technical experts and political leaders to deal with a more complex and imperfect reality. The post-war democratization of higher education has produced a citizenry too sophisticated and critical to accept such preachments. And the flood of information produced by the media and computer revolutions has already breached the information barriers that might have once permitted the maintenance of separate realities for policy makers and the public they serve.

What is needed is not just a revival of citizenship education, but its reformulation to give citizens an accurate picture of complicated reality which is *both* intelligible *and* bearable.

Rendering a complex and intractable world emotionally intelligible to the public will require some of us in education to divert energies from specialized research and the generation of new knowledge to an on-going process of collecting, summarizing, and simplifying the most important portions of the flood of new information produced by others—and to the task of presenting that information in ways that are understandable to the average citizen.

Rendering a complex and intractable world emotionally bearable will require introducing citizens to the concept of the genuine dilemma—the frequent necessity in political life of choosing among equally legitimate but conflicting values and interests, when more of one good thing necessarily means less of another. It will also require judging the performance of the American system not only against what is *ideal*, but also against what is apparently *possible*—in light of the historical attempts of others to cope with similar problems and in light of the performance of other contemporary governments.

No amount of citizenship education can eliminate the frustration that the end of abundance will generate, or the disruption that accelerating technological and social change will cause. But an improved public understanding of the complexity of reality and of the inevitability of trade-offs might help maintain a balance between the democratic advantages of self-criticism and reform and a public appreciation of what is good about the American system.

Inasmuch as this closing chapter has been concerned with placing the collaborative movement within a context of wide-ranging projections about the direction of American society, economy, and education, it is perhaps appropriate to close with another prediction. The absence of citizenship education, in the sense just described, will be the next deficiency of the American education system to be proclaimed a "crisis." It might not be a bad idea for some of us to begin dealing with that problem, now.

William T. Daly is professor of political science at Stockton State College, chairman of the New Jersey Task Force on Thinking Skills, and the founder and director of the Stockton Connection collaborative.

This chapter provides sources of additional assistance.

Additional Resources

William T. Daly

The most comprehensive single source for information on collaboratives is the Council of Articulated Programs. (Contact: Janet Lieberman, LaGuardia Community College, 31-10 Thomson Ave., Long Island, N.Y. 11101, (718) 626-8740.)

Below, however, is a highly selective list of particularly interesting and successful collaboratives. They are grouped as examples of the same major approaches to collaboration as those discussed in this volume.

Early Identification and Support

The PRIME program of the Philadelphia Public Schools provides early identification and support for promising students in math and science. (Contact: Alexander Tobin, School District of Philadelphia, Division of Math Education, 21st St., South, Philadelphia, Pa. 19103, (215) 299-7811.)

The Select Program in Science and Engineering at City College of New York provides Saturday instruction and career counseling for minority students interested in engineering. (Contact: Alfred Posamentier, Department of Secondary and Continuing Education, CCNY, Covenant Avenue at 138th St., New York, N.Y., 10031, (212) 690-5471.)

William T. Daly. *College-School Collaboration: Appraising the Major Approaches.* New Directions for Teaching and Learning, no. 24. San Francisco: Jossey-Bass, December 1985.

Early Instruction in the High Schools

The School-College Articulation Program at Kenyon College works with high school teachers in both rural and urban districts who then teach college courses in their own high schools. (Contact: Joan Straumonis, Academic Dean, Kenyon College, Gambier, Oh. 43022, (614) 427-2244.)

Early Instruction by the College

The University of Maryland's Short Courses for Academically Talented Students provide special summer courses for talented students in the seventh through twelfth grade (Contact: Faith Gabelnick, General Honors Program, University of Maryland, 0110 Hornbake Library, College Park, Md. 20742, (301) 454-2535.)

Combining High School and College

Simon's Rock of Bard College provides an accelerated program for able students which combines the last two years of high school with two or four years of college. (Contact: Eileen Handelman, Dean of the College, Simon's Rock of Bard College, Great Barrington, Mass. 01230, (413) 528-0771.)

The Clarkson School's Bridging Year Program provides college instruction for able students in science, math, and engineering, who have completed the eleventh grade. (Contact: Gary F. Kelly, Clarkson School, Clarkson College of Technology, Potsdam, N.Y. 13676, (315) 268-6400.)

Working with Teachers

The Brown University Teaching Project provides two-day institutes and opportunities for follow-up to Providence high school teachers on topics of their choice. (Contact: Robert Shaw, Assistant Dean of the College, Brown University, P.O. Box 1975, Providence, R.I. 02912, (401) 863-2315.)

The Learning Bridge involves on-going professional and curricular development work between faculty at San Francisco State University and Balboa High School. (Contact: Laura Head, Coordinator, Learning Bridge Project, San Francisco State University, 1600 Holloway Avenue, North Administration Building 445, San Francisco, Calif. 94132, (415) 469-2073.)

The National Humanities Faculty, founded in 1968, has maintained a successful national collaborative program for over fifteen years. It carries out various humanities projects in a variety of schools by identifying a corps of exceptional college and university teachers to work with the school teachers and administrators. (Contact: Benjamin Ladner, Director, National Humanities Faculty, 1735 Lowergate Drive, Atlanta, Ga. 30322, (404) 329-5788.)

Association Activity

In additon to national associations supporting school-college collaborations mentioned in the preceding chapters, the American Association of Higher Education devoted its 1984 national meeting to this theme. It continues its interest in school-college partnerships. (Contact: Lou Albert, Director of Special Projects, American Association of Higher Education, One Dupont Circle, Suite 600, Washington, D.C. 20036.)

William T. Daly is professor of political sience at Stockton State College, chairman of the New Jersey Task Force on Thinking Skills, and the founder and director of the Stockton Connection collaborative.

Index

A

Academic Alliances Program: analysis of, 3, 69–78; described, 70–71; evaluation of, 76–77; incentive and funding for, 75–76; meetings of, 71–72; recommendations from, 77–78; starting, 73–75
Advanced Placement, 28, 33, 44
Alaska, writing project in, 64
Albert, L., 123
American Association of Higher Education, 1, 123
American Historical Association, 76
Australia, writing project in, 63

B

Bailey, A. Y., 81
Balboa High School, Learning Bridge of, 122
Bard College, Simon's Rock of, 122
Bay Area Writing Project, 61, 63, 64, 65, 66, 67, 68
Benbow, C. P., 38, 46
Board of Education (New York City), 48
Board of Higher Education (New Jersey), 7
Board of Higher Education (New York City), 48
Boyer, E. L., 48, 56, 79, 85, 88
Brown University, Teaching Project at, 122

C

California: early identification and support of students in, 19–25; writing project in, 64
California at Berkeley, University of: MESA program at, 2, 19–23; and writing network, 62, 64–65
Canada, writing network in, 63

Carnegie Commission on Higher Education, 28, 35
Carnegie Corporation of New York, 22, 48, 68
Carnegie Foundation for the Advancement of Teaching, 1, 79, 87
Center for the Advancement of Academically Talented Youth (CTY): analysis of, 3, 37–46; background on, 37–38; described, 38–39, 42–43; evaluation of, 42–45; objectives of, 41–42; origin of, 39–41; personnel for, 44, 45; recommendations from, 45–46; and Talent Search, 38, 42
Chao, C. I., 35
Chapman, D. W., 31, 33, 35, 36
Chicago, University of, and Middle College, 47
City College of New York, Select Program in Science and Engineering at, 121
City University of New York, 9, 14; and Middle College, 48
Clarkson College of Technology, Bridging Year Program at, 122
Classroom Behavior Survey, 33
Coalition of 100 Black Women, 107
Collaboration: in academic alliances, 69–78; and citizenship, 117–119; for combined school and college, 47–57, 122; for content updating, 91–97; and crisis in education, 113–119; for early identification and support of students, 19–25; for early instruction, 27–46; and economic prosperity, 117; for empowering teachers, 79–89; future for, 113–119; and individual opportunity, 115–116; interest in, 1; in national network, 61–68; need for, 5–15; opportunity for, 113–114; overview of, 2–4; purposes of, 1–2; resources on 121–123; and roots of crisis, 114–115; and skills testing, 7–15; starting, 99–109; with students, 19–57; with teachers, 59–97
College Board, 8, 42, 44, 81

Y

Yale-New Haven Teachers Institute:
analysis of, 3, 79-89; evaluation of,
85-86; financing, 85; principles of,
82-85; recommendations from,
86-88; and self-interest, 81-82; and
teacher preparation, 79-80; and
urban education, 80-81